THE WAR PO
WILFRED OWEN

Owen's draft Preface (reproduced by permission of the British Library). See p.98 for a transcription.

THE WAR POEMS
OF WILFRED OWEN

Edited and Introduced by
Jon Stallworthy

Chatto & Windus
LONDON

Published in 1994 by
Chatto & Windus Limited
20 Vauxhall Bridge Road London SW1V 2SA

Reprinted 2000, 2001, 2002, 2003,
2005, 2006, 2007 (twice), 2008 (twice), 2009,
2010 (twice), 2016 (twice), 2017 (twice)

A CIP catalogue record for this book is available from
the British Library

ISBN 978 0 7011 6126 2

Phototypeset by
SX Composing Ltd, Rayleigh, Essex

Penguin Random House is committed to a sustainable future for
our business, our readers and our planet. This book is made from
Forest Stewardship Council® certified paper.

Printed and bound in Great Britain by Clays Ltd, St Ives plc

FOREWORD

This edition makes available to the student and general reader the texts and notes of 46 poems and 11 fragments published in the two-volume *Complete Poems and Fragments* (1983). That work sought to establish the texts and the chronology of all Owen's surviving poems and fragments, to chart their manuscripts, and to offer such factual (as distinct from interpretative) notes as the reader might need to understand them. In that endeavour, it built upon foundations laid by previous editors – Mr Siegfried Sassoon (assisted by Dame Edith Sitwell), Professor Edmund Blunden, Mr Cecil Day Lewis, and Dr Dominic Hibberd – to the last of whom I owed a particular debt. Dr Hibberd had been at work on a critical study, *Owen the Poet* (1986), while I was editing the texts, and he was more than generous in sharing his solutions of our common problems.

Editions of this kind necessarily bring together the work and insights of many people, and I should like to record especial gratitude to the editors of the *Collected Letters*, Mr John Bell and the late Harold Owen, Dr Cathrael Kazin who transcribed and dated many of the manuscripts, Miss Catharine Carver the paragon of publishers' editors, and, last but not least, my wife who so good-naturedly and for so long accepted Wilfred Owen as a ghostly addition to the family.

Wolfson College   J.H.S.
Oxford
August 1993

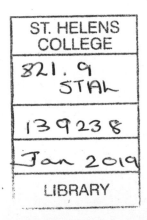

CONTENTS

Dates of composition and revision will be found under
the texts of individual poems

1893 *18 March* Wilfred Edward Salter Owen (WO) born at Plas
Wilmot, Oswestry, son of Tom and Susan Owen

1895 *30 May* Mary Millard Owen born

1897 *16 March* Plas Wilmot sold at Grandfather Shaw's death.
Tom Owen appointed to supervisory post at Birkenhead with
the Great Western and London and North Eastern Railways
April Tom Owen applies for transfer; appointed to
Shrewsbury
5 September Harold Owen (HO) born in Canon Street,
Shrewsbury

1897–8 *Winter* Tom Owen reappointed to Birkenhead. Family
moves to 14 Willmer Road, Birkenhead

1898 *Spring* Holiday in Ireland

1898–9 Move to 7 Elm Grove, Birkenhead, and further move to 51
Milton Street, Birkenhead

1900 *11 June* WO starts school (in mid-term) at the Birkenhead
Institute
24 July Colin Shaw Owen (CO) born

1902 *Summer* Holiday at Tramore, Ireland

1903
or *Summer* Holiday in Broxton
1904

1905 Summer Holiday in Scarborough
August Holiday with the Paton family at Rhewl, Wales

1906 *July* Holiday at Torquay and Carbis Bay
Summer Holiday with the Smallpage family at Waenfawr,
Wales

1906–7 *Winter* Tom Owen appointed Assistant Superintendent, GW
and LNER, Western Region; the family moves to 1
Cleveland Place, Underdale Road, Shrewsbury. WO starts at
Shrewsbury Technical School

1908 *April* WO stays with the Gunston family in Wimbledon
June Tom Owen takes WO to Brittany

1909 *July* WO goes again to Brittany with his father, then to
Torquay

1910 *January* The family moves to Mahim, Monkmoor Road, Shrewsbury

August WO and HO on holiday in Torquay. WO calls on Miss Christabel Coleridge, granddaughter of the poet

1911 *April* WO again on holiday in Torquay; reads Sidney Colvin's *Keats* and visits Teignmouth

Summer Works as a pupil-teacher at the Wyle Cop School, Shrewsbury, while preparing for matriculation exam

9 September Takes University of London matriculation exam. Visits British Museum to see Keats manuscripts

28 September Interview with the Revd Herbert Wigan, vicar of Dunsden, near Reading. Is offered an unpaid post as lay assistant and pupil in this Evangelical parish

Early October Hears he has matriculated, but not with honours

20 October Arrives at Dunsden

1912 *16 April* Arranges to take botany classes at University College, Reading, for six hours a week

June Meets Miss Edith Morley, head of the English Department, University College

8 July Joins family at Pringle Bank, Kelso, for holiday with the Bulman family

20–25 July Attends Keswick Convention

December Miss Morley urges him to sit for a scholarship to University College, Reading, and invites him to attend her remaining classes in Old English free of charge

Christmas At Shrewsbury

28 December Visits Mr Morgan, a clergyman at Bordesley, Birmingham, and is offered another post as lay assistant, which he does not accept. Returns to Dunsden

1913 *Early January* Determines to leave Dunsden and to break with Evangelical religion

7 February Returns to Shrewsbury

February–March Ill with congestion of the lungs

13 March HO joins the Merchant Service and sails for the Mediterranean and India

18 April–3 May Convalescent holiday in Torquay. Starts to look for teaching post

16–19 May Takes the Reading University scholarship

July HO returns to England

c 6 July Hears he has failed to win the Reading scholarship

August Holiday with Uncle Edward Quayle's family at Dorfold, Great Meols, Cheshire

c 15 September To Bordeaux, to teach English at the Berlitz School of Languages. Lodges in rue Castelmoron

28 September Moves into room at 95 rue Porte Dijeaux

Mid-October Visited in Bordeaux by Tom Owen

November Ill with gastro-enteritis

1913–14 *Winter* HO again at sea in the South Atlantic, remaining at sea, with occasional short leaves, until autumn 1916

1914 *18 March* Twenty-first birthday

25 July Gives up job at the Berlitz School

31 July To Castel Lorenzo, Bagnères-de-Bigorre, High Pyrenees, as tutor to Mme Léger, a Berlitz pupil

4 August War declared. French government moves to Bordeaux

c 21 August Meets the poet Laurent Tailhade

24 August Invited by Mme Léger to go with her to Canada in March 1915

17 September Returns to Bordeaux with the Légers, and stays with them at 12 rue Blanc-Dutrouilh. Starts to look for pupils as a freelance teacher of English

2 October Moves to temporary lodgings with the family of a pupil, Raoul Lem, at 12 rue St Louis, Bordeaux

12 October Mme Léger leaves for Canada

19 October Moves to new lodgings at 31 rue Desfourniels

4 December Offered post as tutor to the two elder de la Touche boys at the Châlet, Mérignac, near Bordeaux

8 December Accepts post for a month, retaining his private pupils and going to Mérignac in the afternoons

19 December Moves to Mérignac to live at the Châlet

1915 *Early January* Channel considered unsafe. Invited to stay at Mérignac until the spring

10 April Miss de la Touche, the boys' aunt, decides to keep them in France and urges WO to stay

18 May To Imperial Hotel, Russell Square, London, while carrying out a commission at the British Industries Fair for a Bordeaux scent manufacturer, then to Shrewsbury for a short visit

13 June Returns to Bordeaux via Le Havre and Paris. Into new lodgings at 18 rue Beaubadat, continuing to teach the de la Touche boys as well as his Bordeaux pupils

20 June Considers joining the Artists' Rifles in the autumn, after returning the boys to Downside School

10 July Considers joining the Italian Cavalry if he is unable to join the Artists' Rifles

31 August Gives up lodgings to return to England; persuaded to stay on three more weeks, and finds new lodgings at 1 Place St Christoly, Bordeaux

14 September To London with Johnny and Bobbie de la Touche

15 September Sees the boys off to Downside from Paddington and goes home to Shrewsbury

21 October Joins up in the Artists' Rifles. Into lodgings at Les Lilas, 54 Tavistock Square, WC1

27 October Meets Harold Monro at the Poetry Bookshop, 35 Devonshire Street, W1

15 November To Hare Hall Camp, Gidea Park, Essex, as Cadet Owen, Artists' Rifles

1916 *c 1 January* Home on a week's leave

27 February–5 March Ten days' course in London; lodgings over the Poetry Bookshop

4 March Shows poems to Monro

5 March To Officers' School, Balgores House, Gidea Park

19 May On leave, first in London and then in Shrewsbury, pending gazette

4 June Commissioned into the Manchester Regiment

18 June Reports to 5th (Reserve) Battalion, Manchester Regiment, at Milford Camp, near Witley, Surrey

7 July Attached for a musketry course to 25th Battalion, Middlesex Regiment, Talavera Barracks, Aldershot

Mid-July Weekend leave at Kidmore End, near Reading, home of cousin Leslie Gunston (ELG). To church at Dunsden and sees Revd Wigan

Early August To Mytchett Musketry Camp, Farnborough, in command of the 5th Manchesters contingent

Early September Applies for transfer to Royal Flying Corps, interviewed in London, but is not transferred

14 September Visit from HO

24 September 5th Manchesters move to Oswestry, under canvas

19–20 October 5th Manchesters to Southport, Lancashire, the officers in Queen's Hotel. WO has lodgings for a few days at 168a Lord Street

c 5 November To the firing ranges at Fleetwood in command of the battalion and brigade firing parties. Lodgings at 111 Bold Street, Fleetwood

8 December Back to Southport

Christmas Embarkation leave

29 December To France and Base Camp, Étaples

1917 *1–2 January* Joins 2nd Manchesters on the Somme near Beaumont Hamel, in a rest area. Assumes command of 3 Platoon, A Company

6 January 2nd Manchesters on the move towards front

9–16 January Holds dug-out in no man's land; sentry blinded

20 January Into line again; platoon exposed in severe frost

4 February Arrives at Abbeville for a course on transport duties

25 February leaves Abbeville

1 March Rejoins battalion near Fresnoy; posted to B Company

14/15 March Concussion following fall at Le Quesnoy-en-Santerre

15 March Evacuated to Military Hospital at Nesle

17 March Moved to 13th Casualty Clearing Station at Gailly

4 April Rejoins battalion at Selency

8 April Battalion is relieved, and pulls back to Beauvois

12 April Into the line again at Savy Wood for 12 days

21 April 14th Brigade relieved; into cellar quarters at Quivières

2 May Evacuated to 13th CCS with shell-shock

11 June To No. 1 General Hospital, Etretat

16 June To Welsh Hospital, Netley, Hampshire

26 June Arrives at Craiglockhart War Hospital, Slateford, near Edinburgh

Early July Visited by Susan Owen

17 July Writes first contribution to *The Hydra*; becomes editor

Late July Siegfried Sassoon (SS) arrives at Craiglockhart

30 July Talks to 'Field Club' on 'Do Plants Think?'

c 17 August Introduces himself to SS

1 September 'Song of Songs' published in *The Hydra*

25 September Gives first of several lessons in English literature at Tynecastle School, Edinburgh; appears before Medical Board

13 October Introduced by SS to Robert Graves, who is shown draft of 'Disabled'

28 October Appears before Medical Board; three weeks' leave pending return to unit

3 November To London

4 November To Shrewsbury

9 November Lunches and dines with Robert Ross at the Reform Club and meets Arnold Bennett and H. G. Wells

10 November Dines again with Ross, Wells, and Bennett and meets A. G. Gardiner, editor of the *Daily News*

11 November Visits ELG near Winchester

14 November Sees Monro at the Poetry Bookshop

24 November Joins 5th Manchesters at Scarborough for light duties; appointed 'major-domo' of the Officers' Mess, Clarence Gardens Hotel

4 December Promoted Lieutenant

19–23 December Short leave; to Edinburgh, revisiting Craiglockhart and Tynecastle School

Christmas SS posted back to France

1918 *23 January* Attends Graves's marriage to Nancy Nicholson at St James's Piccadilly. Meets Charles Scott Moncrieff

26 January 'Miners' published in *The Nation*

12 March To Northern Command Depot, Ripon

c 23 March Rents a room at 7 Borrage Lane, Ripon

9–11 April Weekend leave in Shrewsbury and last meeting with HO

22 April Upgraded to Division 4

10 May Upgraded to Division 3

Mid-May 'Song of Songs' published in *The Bookman*

16–19 May In London, staying in flat over Ross's in Half Moon Street. Visits War Office; meets Osbert Sitwell at Ross's flat

21 May Upgraded to Division 2

4 June Graded fit for general service

5 June Rejoins 5th Manchesters at Scarborough

11 June Request from Edith and Osbert Sitwell for poems to include in *Wheels 1918*

15 June 'Hospital Barge' and 'Futility' published in *The Nation*

Mid-June CO joins the RAF

13 July SS wounded and invalided home

Mid-July HO sails to join the light cruser *Astraea* at Simonstown

12–18 August Embarkation leave; sees SS in hospital in London; spends evening with SS and Osbert Sitwell

31 August Reports again to Base Camp, Étaples

9 September To Reception Depot, Amiens, to await arrival of 2nd Manchesters

15 September 2nd Manchesters arrive at Amiens

29 September–3 October Successful assault on Beaurevoir-Fonsomme line. Awarded MC

5 October Battalion back to rest area at Hancourt. Robert Ross dies in London

29 October At St Souplet, into line for the last time

30–31 October Battalion takes over the line west of the Oise-Sambre Canal, near Ors, in preparation for an attack across the canal at dawn on 4 November

4 November Killed in early morning on the canal bank

11 November News of WO's death reaches Shrewsbury. Armistice signed

LIST OF ABBREVIATIONS

WO	Wilfred Owen	ELG	Leslie Gunston
CDL	C. Day Lewis	HO	Harold Owen (brother)
CO	Colin Owen (brother)	MO	Mary Owen (sister)
CU	Columbia University	OS	Osbert Sitwell
	Library Manuscript	SO	Susan Owen (mother)
DH	Dominic Hibberd	SS	Siegfried Sassoon
EB	Edmund Blunden		

PRINCIPAL PUBLISHED SOURCES
By Wilfred Owen:

CDL *The Collected Poems of Wilfred Owen*, edited with an Introduction and Notes by C. Day Lewis (London, 1963)

CL *Wilfred Owen / Collected Letters*, edited by Harold Owen and John Bell (London, 1967)

CP&F *Wilfred Owen / The Complete Poems and Fragments*, edited by Jon Stallworthy (London, 1983)

DH *Wilfred Owen / War Poems and Others*, edited with an Introduction and Notes by Dominic Hibberd (London, 1973)

EB *The Poems of Wilfred Owen*, edited with a Memoir by Edmund Blunden (London, 1931)

JS *The Poems of Wilfred Owen*, edited and introduced by Jon Stallworthy (London, 1985)

SS Wilfred Owen, *Poems*, with an Introduction by Siegfried Sassoon (London, 1920)

OTHER SOURCES

Bäckman Sven Bäckman, *Tradition Transformed / Studies in the Poetry of Wilfred Owen* (Lund, Sweden, 1979)

JFO Harold Owen, *Journey from Obscurity*, 3 vols (London, 1963–5)
N&Q *Notes and Queries*
RES *Review of English Studies*
Welland Dennis Welland, *Wilfred Owen / A Critical Study*, revised and enlarged edition (London, 1978)
WO Jon Stallworthy, *Wilfred Owen* (London, 1974)

All other sources are given in full in the text.

INTRODUCTION

Orpheus, the pagan saint of poets, went through hell and came back singing. In twentieth-century mythology, the singer wears a steel helmet and makes his descent 'down some profound dull tunnel' in the stinking mud of the Western Front. For most readers of English poetry, the face under the helmet is that of Wilfred Owen.

EARLY YEARS

Wilfred Edward Salter Owen was born in Oswestry on 18 March 1893. His parents were then living in a spacious and comfortable house owned by his grandfather, Edward Shaw. At his death two years later, this former mayor of the city was found to be almost bankrupt, and Tom Owen was obliged to move with his wife and son to lodgings in the back streets of Birkenhead. They carried with them vivid memories of their vanished prosperity, and Susan Owen resolved that her adored son should in time restore the family to its rightful gentility. She was a devout Evangelical Christian and, under her strong influence, Wilfred grew into a serious and slightly priggish boy. He started school at seven, and two or three years later discovered his vocation during an idyllic Cheshire holiday with his mother (who had left her other children, Mary, Harold and Colin, with their father): 'At Broxton, by the Hill', he wrote, 'was born . . . my poethood.'

Early in 1907, the family moved to Shrewsbury where Tom Owen had been appointed Assistant Superintendent of the Joint Railways. Wilfred went to the Shrewsbury Technical School and worked hard and successfully, especially at botany and English literature. His interest in poetry (particularly that of Keats) was growing, but still exceeded by his preoccupation with religion. Every day he read a passage from the Bible appointed by the Scripture Union, with the aid of its notes, and sometimes on Sundays would rearrange his parents' sitting-room to represent a church. Then, wearing a linen surplice and cardboard mitre made by his mother, he would summon the family to an evening service complete with sermon.

He was also developing outdoor interests. With his cousins Vera and Leslie Gunston, he formed an Astronomical, Geological and Botanical Society (of three members). As his enthusiasm for botany had led him to the study of geology, so this in turn led him to archaeology and, in 1909, he made the first of many expeditions to the site of the Roman city of Uriconium at Wroxeter, east of Shrewsbury. He left school in

1911, eager to go to university, and passed the University of London matriculation exam, though not with the first-class honours necessary to win him the scholarship he needed. Disappointed, he accepted the offer of an unpaid position as lay assistant to the Rev. Herbert Wigan, Vicar of Dunsden, a village outside Reading. In return for help with his parish duties, Wigan was to give him free board and lodging and some tuition to prepare him for the university entrance exam. The arrangement was not a success. Wigan had no interest in literature, and Owen soon lost interest in theology, the only topic offered for tuition. Over the coming months, however, he attended botany classes at University College, Reading, and was encouraged both in his writing and in his literary studies by the Head of the English department. Meanwhile, influenced by his reading of Shelley, atheist and revolutionary (whom he was happy to learn had lived nearby), as well as the Gospels, he gave practical help to the poor of the parish. His letters home show the first signs of the compassion that would characterize his poems from the Western Front:

> I am increasingly liberalizing my thought, spite of the Vicar's strong Conservatism. And when he paws his beard, and wonders whether £10. is too high a price for new curtains for the dining room, (in place of the faded ones you saw); then the fires smoulder ... From what I hear straight from the tight-pursed lips of wolfish ploughmen in their cottages, I might say there is material for another revolution. Perhaps men will strike, not with absence from work; but with arms at work. Am I for or against upheaval? I know not; I am not happy in these thoughts; yet they press heavy upon me. I am happier when I go to 'distribute dole
> To poor sick people, richer in His eyes,
> Who ransomed us, and haler too than I.

The Vicar had been praying for a religious revival in the parish and, early in 1913, it arrived like a spring tide, sweeping converts into church – but leaving Owen stranded on the recognition that literature meant more to him than evangelical religion. He had to explain this to the Vicar, who was strongly disapproving both of his assistant's altered priorities and of his warm (but probably innocuous) friendship with one of the village boys. Owen's letters to his mother record a developing crisis:

> Escape from this hotbed of religion I now long for more than

I could ever have conceived a year and three months ago . . .

To leave Dunsden will mean a terrible bust-up; but I have no intention of sneaking away by smuggling my reasons down the back-stairs. I will vanish in thunder and lightening, if I go at all.

Go he did, in February 1913, on the verge of a nervous breakdown and with congestion of the lungs that kept him in bed for more than a month. In July he sat a scholarship exam for University College, Reading, but failed, and in mid-September crossed the Channel to take up a part-time post teaching English at the Berlitz School in Bordeaux. Over the next two years, he grew to love France, its language and its literature, and had reached perhaps the highest point of happiness that life would offer him, tutoring an eleven-year-old French girl in her parents' Pyrenean villa, when, on 4 August 1914, Germany invaded Belgium and war was declared.

EARLY INFLUENCES AND POEMS

The earliest and probably the most important literary influence on Wilfred Owen (as on so many other writers in English) was the Bible. This he would have heard read aloud before he could read it for himself: reading it then under his mother's direction, and that of the Scripture Union notes, he acquired the habit of 'close reading' that would stand him in good stead when he came to literary texts. The fact that he ascribed the birth of his 'poethood' to his Broxton holiday of 1903 or 1904 suggests that he was there introduced to poetry. If so, it was almost certainly Keats's poetry, clearly audible behind his own first attempts at writing verse. The earliest of these to survive was probably 'To Poesy'* (an ironical beginning for a poet whose most famous manifesto would declare: 'Above all I am not concerned with Poetry'). This bears a marked resemblance to Keats's 'The Fall of Hyperion', as other of Owen's adolescent poems would acknowledge in their titles and confirm in their texts a debt to the older poet: 'Before reading a Biography of Keats for the first time' ('On First Looking into Chapman's Homer'), 'Sonnet Written at Teignmouth, on a pilgrimage to Keats's house' ('Sonnet Written in the Cottage where Burns was Born'), and 'On seeing a Lock of Keats' Hair' ('On Seeing a Lock of Milton's Hair').

* This and other of Owen's poems not included in this selection can be found in *The Poems of Wilfred Owen*, ed. Jon Stallworthy, 1985.

Influenced perhaps by Keats's dictum that 'A long poem is a test of Invention, which I take to be the polar star of poetry, as Fancy is the sails, and Imagination the rudder', Owen at Dunsden produced a verse rendering of Hans Andersen's fairy tale 'The Little Mermaid'. His mother would have approved of this particular tale: a romantic story of sacrificial love and acute bodily suffering nobly borne, it offered scope for those painterly descriptions of physical beauty that he so enjoyed. A mermaid heroine would have appealed to an admirer of Keats's 'Lamia', and he chose the eight-line stanza of 'Isabella'. The texture of the verse is markedly Keatsian and moves with ease and assurance through its seventy-seven stanzas. One, describing the approach of a storm, contains an image and an onomatopoeic use of language that anticipates the later poems from the Western Front:

> It is late. Starry lamps and fierce fusees
> Fade out. The stunning guns are dumb. All ears
> Hark to a grumbling in the heart of the seas.

If Keats was the first object of Owen's lifelong tendency to hero-worship, Shelley was the second. In January 1912 he wrote of 'Shelley, the brightest genius of his time', and Shelley's long poem, *The Revolt of Islam*, may well have awakened Owen's political awareness with its ardent defence of freedom in the face of oppression. Later in 1912, he attended the double funeral of a Dunsden mother and her four-year-old daughter, and responded to that village tragedy with a poem in which his compassion for victims makes itself heard for the first time:

> Deep under turfy grass and heavy clay
> They laid her bruisèd body and the child.
> Poor victims of a swift mischance were they,
> Adown Death's trapdoor suddenly beguiled.

Owen gazes into their open grave with something of the same awed fascination that prompted a more ambitious poem some months later. 'Uriconium/An Ode' (p. 3) is, in an important sense, his first 'war poem'. Contemplating the excavated ruins of the Roman city which, with its inhabitants (his guidebook told him), 'perished by fire and sword', the twenty-year-old poet warms to his subject:

> For here lie remnants from a banquet-table,
> – Oysters and marrow-bones, and seeds of grape –

> The statement of whose age must sound a fable;
> And Samian jars, whose sheen and flawless shape
>   Look fresh from potter's mould.
> Plasters with Roman finger-marks impressed;
> Bracelets, that from the warm Italian arm
>   Might seem to be scarce cold;
> And spears – the same that pushed the Cymry west,
> Unblunted yet . . .

Owen's compassionate awareness of the victims' *bodies* – so prominent a feature of his later and greater poems – enables him to feel those

> Plasters with Roman *finger-marks* impressed;
> Bracelets, that from the *warm Italian arm*
>   Might seem to be *scarce cold*;

and it sharpens his perceptions of the weapons that killed them – 'spears . . . *unblunted* yet'.

  In this poem, Owen set himself

> To lift the gloomy curtain of Time Past
> And spy the secret things that Hades hath,

and other of his early writings reveal a similar fascination with gloom, darkness, and 'secret things'. Telling his mother, for example, of the sequel to a 'violent side-slip' on his bicycle, he wrote: 'I was washing some of the dirt out of the wound, & had applied some of my Carbolic Ointment, when sudden twilight seemed to fall upon the world, an horror of great darkness closed around me.' Dr Hibberd suggests that it may have been the Rev. Wigan who, shortly before Owen's departure from Dunsden, drew his attention to the Epistle of St Jude, a thunderous denunciation of 'certain men crept in unawares' among the faithful, 'filthy dreamers' who corrupt the Church, 'Raging waves of the sea, foaming out their own shame; wandering stars, to whom is reserved the blackness of darkness for ever'. This text, conflated with the last stanza of Shelley's 'Adonais', would find its way into a poem of Owen's, 'O World of Many Worlds'. In this, the speaker desires

> To be a meteor, fast, eccentric, lone,
>   Lawless; in passage through all spheres,

Warning the earth of wider ways unknown
    And rousing men with heavenly fears . . .

This is the track reserved for my endeavour
    Spanless the erring way I wend.
Blackness of darkness is my meed for ever?
    And barren plunging without end?

O glorious fear! Those other wandering souls
    High burning through that outer bourne
Are lights unto themselves. Fair aureoles
    Self-radiated there are worn.

The poem has many flaws but, as Dr Hibberd says, it 'represents a very important stage in Owen's development. In defiance of the Bible and the Church, darkness is now welcomed as the environment proper to a poet.' The 'track reserved' for his poetic endeavour is that of a lonely meteor 'Warning the earth'. His prophecy would be fulfilled when, in 1918, drafting a Preface for the book of poems he would never see, he wrote: 'All a poet can do today is warn.'

LATER YEARS

Owen's response to the outbreak of war was surprising and clearly influenced by his conversations with a portly fifty-nine-year-old French aesthete, duellist and poet, Laurent Tailhade, whom he had just met. He wrote to his mother at the end of August 1914:

> I can do no service to anybody by agitating for news or making dole over the slaughter. On the contrary I adopt the perfect English custom of dealing with an offender: a Frenchman duels with him: an Englishman ignores him. I feel my own life all the more precious and more dear in the presence of this deflowering of Europe. While it is true that the guns will effect a little useful weeding, I am furious with chagrin to think that the Minds which were to have excelled the civilization of ten thousand years, are being annihilated – and bodies, the product of aeons of Natural Selection, melted down to pay for political statues. I regret the mortality of the English regulars less than that of the French, Belgian, or even Russian or German armies: because the former are all Tommy Atkins, poor fellows, while the continental armies

are inclusive of the finest brains and temperaments of the land.

A month later, he had rediscovered the compassion he had shown for the poor at Dunsden, the concern for victims' bodies shown in 'Uriconium'. Following a visit to a hospital for the wounded, he wrote to his brother, Harold:

> One poor devil had his shin-bone crushed by a gun-carriage wheel, and the doctor had to twist it about and push it like a piston to get out the pus. Another had a hole right through the knee . . .

Owen's new hero, Tailhade, had written two pacifist pamphlets, but was also a duellist and by the end of 1914 had joined the French Army. Over the next year, Owen's thinking showed similar conflicts and confusion. He considered following Tailhade's example and joining the French Army; then contemplated applying for a Commission in the (British) Artists' Rifles; then thought he would 'like to join the Italian Cavalry; for reasons both aesthetic and poetical'. His delayed decision indicates an understandable reluctance to go to war, but at no point do his letters speak of any principled aversion to fighting. 'Do you know what would hold me together on a battlefield?' he asked his mother. 'The sense that I was perpetuating the language in which Keats and the rest of them wrote!' Finally, returning to England with two of the boys he had been tutoring in Mérignac, near Bordeaux, he said goodbye to his family and, on 21 October 1915, enlisted in the Artists' Rifles.

For the next seven and a half months he was in training, mainly at Hare Hall Camp in Essex. There were two brief but important interludes in London, spent largely at the Poetry Bookshop in Devonshire Street. Its proprietor, Harold Monro, himself a poet and editor of *The Poetry Review*, read his poems and gave him encouraging advice. On 4 June, Owen was commissioned into the Manchester Regiment and underwent further training with its 5th (Reserve) Battalion in various parts of England. He spent Christmas at home on embarkation leave before crossing to France on 29 December and, in the second week of January 1917 (one of the coldest on record), he led his platoon into the battle of the Somme. As he wrote to his mother of one episode:

> My dug-out held 25 men tight packed. Water filled it to a depth of 1 or 2 feet leaving say 4 feet of air.

One entrance had been blown in & blocked.

So far, the other remained.

The Germans knew we were staying there and decided we shouldn't.

Those fifty hours were the agony of my happy life.

Every ten minutes on Sunday afternoon seemed an hour.

I nearly broke down and let myself drown in the water that was now slowly rising over my knees.

Towards 6 o'clock, when, I suppose, you would be going to church the shelling grew less intense and less accurate: so that I was mercifully helped to do my duty and crawl, wade, climb and flounder over No Man's Land to visit my other post. It took me half an hour to move about 150 yards.

In the Platoon on my left the sentries over the dug-out were blown to nothing. One of these poor fellows was my first servant whom I rejected ... If I had kept him he would have lived, for servants don't do Sentry Duty. I kept my own sentries half way down the stairs during the more terrific bombardment. In spite of this one lad was blown down and, I am afraid, blinded.

In the middle of March, Owen fell through a shell-hole into a cellar and was trapped there for three days with only a candle for company. This experience, compounded with the sickness (probably the result of concussion) that followed his escape, no doubt contributed to the dark images of an Underworld in many of his later poems. After a fortnight in a clean hospital bed, he rejoined his Battalion and was involved in fierce fighting; at one point being blown out of the trench in which he was taking cover from an artillery bombardment that had already dismembered a brother officer in a neighbouring trench. Owen escaped unscathed, but these experiences had taken their toll and, on 1 May, he was seen by his Commanding Officer to be behaving strangely. He was probably told to pull himself together (he seems to have sensed an imputation of cowardice) and report to the Battalion Medical Officer, who found him to be shaky and tremulous and his memory confused. In due course, he was diagnosed as suffering from neurasthenia (shell-shock) and invalided back, first to England, then to Craiglockhart War Hospital on the outskirts of Edinburgh.

What many may have perceived as a misfortune was to prove one of the most fortunate events of Owen's short life. He was put under the care of Captain Arthur Brock RAMC, a perceptive doctor, who believed shell-shock to result from broken contact with real life, and sought to re-establish that vital connexion by means of 'work-cure' (or, as he termed it, 'ergotherapy'). He set Owen to write a long poem on Antaeus, son of Earth (in Greek mythology), who was invincible so long as he kept contact with the ground, but was out-wrestled by Hercules who lifted him into the air ('The Wrestlers', p. 90). At his doctor's suggestion, Owen joined the Field Club Brock had started, and gave its members a lecture on 'Do Plants Think?' He contributed to – and soon became editor of – the hospital magazine, *The Hydra*, which would shortly print two of his poems and four by Siegfried Sassoon.

By July 1917, when he arrived at Craiglockhart, Sassoon had the beginnings of a reputation as a poet, as an infantry officer of exceptional courage (recognized by the award of the Military Cross), and as the author of an 'open letter' to his Commanding Officer protesting at the prolongation of the war 'by those who have the power to end it'. This received an airing in the press and the House of Commons, but the War Office effectively smothered his protest by quickly convening a Medical Board that found him in need of medical attention and sent him to Craiglockhart. His book, *The Old Huntsman and Other Poems*, had just been published. Its 'trench sketches' had an overwhelming effect on Owen, who told his mother: 'Shakespeare reads vapid after these.' He introduced himself, and so began one of the most productive of literary friendships. The older poet's advice and encouragement, showing the younger how to channel memories of battle – recurring in obsessive nightmares that were a symptom of shellshock – into poems, complemented Dr Brock's work-cure. Owen's confidence grew, his health returned, and in October a Medical Board decided he was fit for light duties. On 3 November, he had a last supper with Sassoon and took the midnight train to London and the start of three weeks' leave. Sassoon, who had already introduced him to Robert Graves, had also given him an introduction to Robert Ross, who in turn introduced him to some of his literary friends: the novelists Arnold Bennett and H. G. Wells and a number of less well-known figures, several of whom were homosexual, as were Ross and Sassoon themselves. It is clear from Owen's writings that he shared their sexual orientation; but it is debatable whether he ever entered into a physical relationship that, if detected, could have resulted in a prison sentence like that imposed on Oscar Wilde, a relationship that would have horrified his mother, whose good opinion he valued above all others. There is no evidence that he did. What is certain, however, is that Owen and Sassoon wrote more eloquently than other poets of the tragedy of boys killed in battle because they felt that tragedy more acutely, more personally.

In late November, Owen rejoined the 5th Manchesters in Scarborough where, on New Year's Eve, he reviewed his life:

> I am not dissatisfied with my years. Everything has been done in bouts:
>
> Bouts of awful labour at Shrewsbury & Bordeaux; bouts of amazing pleasure in the Pyrenees, and play at Craiglockhart; bouts of religion at Dunsden; bouts of horrible danger on the Somme; bouts of poetry always; of your affection always; of sympathy for the oppressed always.
>
> I go out of this year a Poet, my dear Mother, as which I did not enter it. I am held peer by the Georgians; I am a poet's poet.
>
> I am started. The tugs have left me; I feel the great swelling of the open sea taking my galleon.
>
> Last year, at this time, (it is just midnight, and now is the intolerable instant of the Change) last year I lay awake in a windy tent in the middle of a vast, dreadful encampment. It seemed neither France nor England, but a kind of paddock where the beasts are kept a few days before the shambles. I heard the revelling of the Scotch troops, who are now dead, and who knew they would be dead. I thought of this present night, and whether I should indeed – whether we should indeed – whether you would indeed – but I thought neither long nor deeply, for I am a master of elision.
>
> But chiefly I thought of the very strange look on all faces in that camp; an incomprehensible look, which a man will never see in England, though wars should be in England; nor can it be seen in any battle. But only in Étaples.
>
> It was not despair, or terror, it was more terrible than terror, for it was a blindfold look, and without expression, like a dead rabbit's.
>
> It will never be painted, and no actor will ever seize it. And to describe it, I think I must go back and be with them.

Since the days of his early hero-worship of Sassoon, Owen had come to share his friend's sense of mission, a word with appropriately religious overtones. Though both poets were, by this time, fiercely critical of the role of a Church that had forgotten the biblical commandment 'Thou shalt not kill', both had a fundamentally religious outlook. Owen never lost his belief in the person and teachings of

Christ, and his mother's Evangelical influence no doubt contributed to his conviction that the poet must share the suffering – even the self-sacrifice – of the troops, so that he could bear witness to 'man's inhumanity to man' and, by his testimony, help to promote a negotiated peace settlement.

In December, Sassoon was again posted overseas – first to Palestine, then to France – and, in March, Owen was transferred to 'an awful camp' at Ripon. There he rented an attic room in a nearby cottage to which he could escape when not on duty. In this, over the next three months, he either wrote or revised and completed many of his most powerful poems, including 'Insensibility' (p. 32), 'Strange Meeting' (p. 35), 'Exposure' (p. 71), and 'Futility' (p. 45). In early June, he was graded 'G.S.' (fit for General Service) and rejoined the 5th Manchesters at Scarborough. A friend in the War Office, Charles Scott Moncrieff, recommended him for a home posting – as instructor to a cadet battalion – but the recommendation was rejected. By then, however, Sassoon had been shot in the head and invalided home, and Owen seems to have accepted that it was his duty as a poet to take his place. 'Now must I throw my little candle on his torch,' he told his mother, 'and go out again.'

The great German offensives of March and April 1918 had exhausted the attackers and, in mid-July, they launched what was to prove their last offensive. This had been contained and their armies were retreating when, at the end of August, Owen returned to France. A month later, he led a platoon of the 2nd Manchesters in the British Army's assault on the German's Beaurevoir-Fonsomme line. Of his experiences on 1 and 2 October, he wrote to his mother:

> I lost all my earthly faculties, and fought like an angel.
>
> If I started into detail of our engagement I should disturb the censor and my own Rest.
>
> You will guess what has happened when I say I am now Commanding the Company, and in the line had a boy lance-corporal as my Sergeant-Major.
>
> With this corporal who stuck to me and shadowed me like your prayers I captured a German Machine Gun and scores of prisoners.
>
> I'll tell you exactly how another time. I only shot one man with my revolver (at about 30 yards!); The rest I took with a smile. The same thing happened with other parties all along the line we entered.

I have been recommended for the Military Cross; and have recommended every single N.C.O. who was with me!

> My nerves are in perfect order.
> I came out in order to help these boys – directly by leading them as well as an officer can; indirectly, by watching their sufferings that I may speak of them as well as a pleader can. I have done the first.

He had in fact done both. He was awarded the Military Cross, and the imputation that he was 'unfit to command troops', which had haunted him since April 1917, was answered with two words and a white and purple ribbon. He did not live to wear this, or to see in print most of the poems that would make his name.

All along the Western Front the Germans were falling back, but they were still capable of fierce resistance and, on the night of 3/4 November, the 2nd Manchesters were ordered to cross the Sambre and Oise Canal, north of Ors. At 5.45, Owen led his platoon to the west bank, and was helping his men assemble a pontoon bridge under heavy fire from the east bank when (according to survivors contacted by Edmund Blunden) he was hit and killed.

By midday the remnants of the 2nd Manchesters were on the other side of the Canal, having crossed south of Ors. And seven days later, as the guns fell silent on the Western Front, the survivors piled their rifles, took off their helmets, and went to sleep; the living like the dead.

In Shrewsbury, the Armistice bells were ringing when the Owens' front-door bell sounded its small chime, heralding the telegram that Tom and Susan had dreaded for two years.

LATER INFLUENCES AND POEMS

The Owen who left for France in 1913 was a late Romantic descendant of Keats and Shelley, but the Owen who left France to enlist in 1915 was equipped to become a modern poet. The difference – as for Yeats and Eliot before him – was the result of his exposure to contemporary French poetry. His reading of French literature was encouraged and directed by Laurent Tailhade, himself a poet of the so-called 'Decadent' school, whose guiding principle was (in the words of the poet Théophile Gautier) *'L'art pour l'art'* or 'art for art's sake'. Tailhade introduced Owen to the poetry of Verlaine, Flaubert's novels, and the work of many other nineteenth-century French writers who challenged and shocked the beliefs and sensibilities of bourgeois society. Their influence can be detected in such of Owen's poems of 1914–1915 as 'Long Ages Past' and 'Maundy Thursday' with its deliberately shocking conclusion:

> Then I, too knelt before that acolyte,
> Above the crucifix I bent my head:
> The Christ was thin, and cold, and very dead:
> And yet, I bowed, yea, kissed – my lips did cling.
> (I kissed the warm live hand that held the thing.)

Owen would later read and be influenced by the British 'Decadents', Swinburne and Wilde, but no less important to his development as a poet was his friendship, from 1915, with Harold Monro. In March 1916 he showed Monro some of his poems and, as he wrote to his mother: 'he told me what was fresh and clever, and what was second-hand and banal; and what was Keatsian, and what "modern".' Monro, friend and publisher of the poets represented in the annual *Georgian Poetry* anthologies, introduced Owen to contemporary British poetry; gave him good advice about his own and (as author of *Strange Meetings*, 1917) the title of his most famous poem.

Not until August 1917, however, did Owen transcend his early influences and find a language for his experience. He learnt this from Sassoon, who had himself learnt from the example of Thomas Hardy to abandon the old-fashioned 'literary' diction and syntax that had disfigured his first poems about the war. Impressed by the conversational directness of Sassoon's 'trench sketches' and their use of direct speech (learnt from Hardy), Owen soon moved beyond imitation ('The Dead-Beat', p. 31), to find his own voice in 'Anthem for Doomed Youth' (p. 12).

Like many of his poems, this has a double source in his experience of literature and life. Stung by a Prefatory Note to an anthology (quoted on p. 12), he angrily asks: 'What passing-bells for these who die as cattle?' Those who die as cattle in a slaughterhouse die in such numbers that there is no time to give them the trappings of a Christian funeral that Owen remembers from his Dunsden days. Instead, they receive a brutal parody of such a service: 'the stuttering rifles' praying that they will kill them; the 'choirs . . . of shells' wailing as they hunt them down. The bugles may sound the 'Last Post' for them, but they had previously called them to the colours in those same sad shires. So, bitterly but obliquely, Owen assigns to Church and State responsibility for their deaths. The 'turn' (or break) following the 'octave' (the first eight lines) brings the reader home across the Channel, and the 'sestet' (the last six lines) opens with a question paralleling the first: 'What candles may be held to speed them all?' It is a gentler question than 'What passing bells for these who die as cattle?' preparing for the gentler answer that, instead of the parodic rituals offered by rifle, shell, and bugle, those who love the soldiers will mark their death with observances more heart-felt, more permanent, than those prescribed by convention.

Some indication of the nature of Sassoon's contribution to Owen's poetic development can be gained from the fact that the final manuscript draft of this poem contains nine words and several cancellations in the handwriting of the older poet, whose own work would never equal the rich density of meaning and music in these lines. The poem 'Dulce et Decorum Est' (p. 29), begun at about the same time, again owes much to Sassoon – in its graphic depiction of the battlefield and its explosive use of direct speech – and again was triggered by Owen's angry response to another text: in this case, a poem or poems by Jessie Pope (see p. 30). It also repudiates a poem of his own, originally entitled 'The Ballad of Peace and War' (CP & F, pp. 505-6), in which 'The Old Lie' of the Latin quotation is offered as a *truth*:

> Oh it is meet and it is sweet
>> To live in peace with others
> But sweeter still and far more meet
>> To die in war for brothers.

Understandably, Owen abandoned this ballad, but it should be remembered that in 1914 his sentiments were similar to those of Rupert Brooke, but less well expressed. Other of Owen's mature poems have their origins in his adolescent ones, and the extent of his development is seen nowhere more dramatically than in his re-writing of 'Wild with All Regrets' (p. 94) as 'A Terre' (p.65), or that of 'Spells and Incantation' (p. 87) as 'I saw his round mouth's crimson' (p. 17).

The last author to have a significant influence on his work was a Frenchman, Henri Barbusse, whose book, *Le Feu*, he read in its English translation, *Under Fire*, over Christmas at Scarborough in 1917. One of the most brilliant and searing accounts of life and death on the Western Front, it made an immediate impact on Owen and filtered into his poems of this period. For example, a sentence of Barbusse's is transformed in the fragment beginning 'Cramped in that funnelled hole' (p. 89). This vision of 'one of the many mouths of Hell' would be more fully elaborated in 'Miners' (p. 24) and 'Strange Meeting' (p. 35), and can be traced back, by way of 'Uriconium' (p. 3), to the Hell of which Owen heard at his mother's knee. These descents into the Underworld have a curious common denominator. The Dunsden elegy for a mother and child speaks of 'Chaos murky womb'; the landscape of 'The Show' (p. 42) is said to be 'pitted with great pocks and scabs of plagues'; the soldiers 'Cramped in that funnelled hole' (p. 89) watched the yawn 'Of death's jaws, which had all but swallowed them / Stuck in the bottom of his throat of phlegm'; and in 'Strange Meeting' (p. 35), the speaker escapes down a tunnel 'through granites which titanic wars had groined'. In each case, the earth is described in terms of the human body, and in three out of four instances there is a marked sense of physical loathing. This comes strangely, tragically, from a poet whose early poems are full of lyrical descriptions of beautiful bodies and celebrations of the natural world.

Part of the power of many of Owen's mature poems derives from his pioneering use of 'pararhymes': escaped/scooped, groined/groaned. In 'Strange Meeting' (p. 35), from which these examples are taken, the second rhyme is usually lower in pitch than the first, giving the couplet 'a dying fall' that musically reinforces the poem's meaning; the tragedy of the German poet (one manuscript reads 'I was a German conscript, and your friend'), his life cut short by the British poet whom he meets in Hell. In the poem 'Miners' (p. 24), the pitch of the pararhymes rises and falls as the sense moves from grief to happiness and back to grief again:

> The centuries will burn rich loads
>   With which we groaned,
> Whose warmth shall lull their dreaming lids,
>   While songs are crooned;
> But they will not dream of us poor lads,
>   Left in the ground.

In September 1918, Owen returned to the Front, under no illusions about what awaited him. Before going into the trenches he wrote to Sassoon: 'Serenity Shelley never dreamed of crowns me. Will it last when I shall have gone into Caverns & Abysmals such as he never reserved for his worst daemons?' Once again, his image is of Hell. Later that month, remembering his sentry blinded in January 1917, he wrote 'The Sentry' (p. 74). The torrential movement of this poem makes it seem simpler, more straightforward than it is. It begins: 'We'd found an old Boche dug-out, and he knew, / And gave us hell . . . ' The slang figure of speech conceals the recurrent metaphor. Similarly, when Owen speaks of 'one who would have drowned himself for good', he means more than 'once and for all', and may well have had in mind the moment when death by drowning seemed, to him, good and preferable to living (see the letter quoted on p. xxvi above).

In his celebrated draft Preface (p. 98), Owen wrote: 'All a poet can do today is warn. That is why the true Poets must be truthful.' It sounds easy, but it is not easy to tell the truth in a poem, especially a truth from which the memory recoils. He tells the truth in 'The Sentry' when he says: 'I try not to remember these things now'. But, when he tries to forget them, 'Eyeballs, huge-bulged like squids', / Watch my dreams still'. In those dreams the horror is re-born, the reality of battle re-shaped to the dimensions of the poem; poems to which we, his readers, owe – more than to any other – our vision of the reality of the Western Front, of Hell on earth.

TEXTUAL NOTE

The editorial principles underlying the texts of this edition are the same as those set out in full in CP & F and, more briefly, in JS. Under the notes to each poem and fragment, a page reference to CP & F shows where, in volume 2 of that edition, its textual history is to be found.

THE POEMS

URICONIUM
An Ode

It lieth low near merry England's heart
Like a long-buried sin; and Englishmen
Forget that in its death their sires had part.
And, like a sin, Time lays it bare again
5   To tell of races wronged,
And ancient glories suddenly overcast,
And treasures flung to fire and rabble wrath.
         If thou hast ever longed
To lift the gloomy curtain of Time Past,
10 And spy the secret things that Hades hath,
Here through this riven ground take such a view.
The dust, that fell unnoted as a dew,
Wrapped the dead city's face like mummy-cloth:
All is as was: except for worm and moth.

15 Since Jove was worshipped under Wrekin's shade
Or Latin phrase was writ in Shropshire stone,
Since Druid chaunts desponded in this glade
Or Tuscan general called that field his own,
         How long ago? How long?
20 How long since wanderers in the Stretton Hills
Met men of shaggy hair and savage jaw,
         With flint and copper prong,
Aiming behind their dikes and thorny grilles?
         Ah! those were days before the axe and saw,
25   Then were the nights when this mid-forest town
         Held breath to hear the wolves come yelping down,
         And ponderous bears 'long Severn lifted paw,
         And nuzzling boars ran grunting through the shaw.

Ah me! full fifteen hundred times the wheat
30 Hath risen, and bowed, and fallen to human hunger
Since those imperial days were made complete.
The weary moon hath waxen old and younger
         These eighteen thousand times
Without a shrine to greet her gentle ray.
35 And other temples rose; to Power and Pelf,

And chimed centurial chimes
Until their very bells are worn away.
While King by King lay cold on vaulted shelf
And wars closed wars, and many a Marmion fell,
40 And dearths and plagues holp sire and son to hell;
And old age stiffened many a lively elf
And many a poet's heart outdrained itself.

I had forgot that so remote an age
Beyond the horizon of our little sight,
45 Is far from us by no more spanless gauge
Than day and night, succeeding day and night,
      Until I looked on Thee,
Thou ghost of a dead city, or its husk!
But even as we could walk by field and hedge
50   Hence to the distant sea
So, by the rote of common dawn and dusk,
We travel back to history's utmost edge.
Yea, when through thy old streets I took my way,
And recked a thousand years as yesterday,
55 Methought sage fancy wrought a sacrilege
To steal for me such godly privilege!

For here lie remnants from a banquet table –
Oysters and marrow-bones, and seeds of grape –
The statement of whose age must sound a fable;
60 And Samian jars, whose sheen and flawless shape
      Look fresh from potter's mould.
Plasters with Roman finger-marks impressed;
Bracelets, that from the warm Italian arm
      Might seem to be scarce cold;
65 And spears – the same that pushed the Cymry west –
Unblunted yet; with tools of forge and farm
Abandoned, as a man in sudden fear
Drops what he holds to help his swift career:
For sudden was Rome's flight, and wild the alarm.
70 The Saxon shock was like Vesuvius' qualm.

O ye who prate of modern art and craft
Mark well that Gaulish brooch, and test that screw!

[4]

Art's fairest buds on antique stem are graft.
Under the sun is nothing wholly new!
75   At Viricon today
The village anvil rests on Roman base
And in a garden, may be seen a bower
      With pillars for its stay
That anciently in basilic had place.
80 The church's font is but a pagan dower:
A Temple's column, hollowed into this.
So is the glory of our artifice,
Our pleasure and our worship, but the flower
Of Roman custom and of Roman power.

85 O ye who laugh and, living as if Time
Meant but the twelve hours ticking round your dial,
Find it too short for thee, watch the sublime,
Slow, epochal time-registers awhile,
      Which are Antiquities.
90 O ye who weep and call all your life too long
And moan: Was ever sorrow like to mine?
      Muse on the memories
That sad sepulchral stones and ruins prolong.
Here might men drink of wonder like strong wine
95 And feel ephemeral troubles soothed and curbed.
Yet farmers, wroth to have their laws disturbed,
Are sooner roused for little loss to pine
Than we are moved by mighty woes long syne.

Above this reverend ground, what traveller checks?
00 Yet cities such as these one time would breed
Apocalyptic visions of world-wrecks.
Let Saxon men return to them, and heed!
      They slew and burnt,
But after, prized what Rome had given away
05 Out of her strength and her prosperity.
      Have they yet learnt
The precious truth distilled from Rome's decay?
Ruins! On England's heart press heavily!
For Rome hath left us more than walls and words

And better yet shall leave, and more than herds
Or land or gold gave the Celts to us in fee;
E'en Blood, which makes poets sing and prophets see.

Written, probably at Shrewsbury, in July 1913 (WO, 88–90). Since August 1909, and perhaps earlier, WO had been a fascinated explorer of the remains of Uriconium, the Roman city at Wroxeter, on the Severn, east of Shrewsbury. The city and its inhabitants were destroyed by fire and sword *c.* AD 400. The first excavations were carried out in 1859–61, and the more important finds placed in the Shrewsbury Museum. WO and HO themselves collected several boxes full of shards. 'Uriconium/An Ode' owes a good deal to WO's copy of George Fox's *Guide to the Roman City of Uriconium* (1911).

15 Wrekin's shade: The Wrekin is a hill ten miles to the east of
    Shrewsbury.

28 shaw: thicket or small wood.

39 Marmion: Lord Marmion, the hero of Scott's poem, *Marmion/A Tale of
    Flodden Field* (1808), was killed at the battle of Flodden in 1513.

63 Cp. Keats, 'The Eve of St Agnes', l. 228: 'Unclasps her warmed jewels
    one by one'.

65 the Cymry: the Welsh.

70 Vesuvius' qualm: WO owned a copy of Bulwer-Lytton's *The Last Days of
    Pompeii* (1834), and in January 1909 wrote a lurid school essay on the
    subject of earthquakes and volcanic eruptions.

91 Cp. Herbert, 'The Sacrifice', l.4: 'Was ever grief like mine?'

CP&F, 211

[6]

A NEW HEAVEN
(TO ——— ON ACTIVE SERVICE)

Seeing we never found gay fairyland
   (Though still we crouched by bluebells moon by moon)
And missed the tide of Lethe; yet are soon
   For that new bridge that leaves old Styx half-spanned;
5 Nor ever unto Mecca caravanned;
   Nor bugled Asgard, skilled in magic rune;
Nor yearned for far Nirvana, the sweet swoon,
   And from high Paradise are cursed and banned;

– Let's die home, ferry across the Channel! Thus
10   Shall we live gods there. Death shall be no sev'rance.
Weary cathedrals light new shrines for us.
   To us, rough knees of boys shall ache with rev'rence.
Are not girls' breasts a clear, strong Acropole?
– There our own mothers' tears shall heal us whole.

Written probably at Witley and, according to one dated MS, in September 1916.

TITLE Taken from Revelation 31:1, 'And I saw a new heaven and a new earth: for the first heaven and the first earth were passed away.'

DEDICATION The unnamed soldier has not been identified.

3 Lethe: In Greek mythology, a river through Hades the taste of whose waters caused forgetfulness of the past.

4 Styx: In Greek mythology, the boundary river encircling Hades.

6 Asgard: In Norse mythology, the abode of the gods, accessible only by the bridge Bifrost.

9 The MS reads: '– Let's die home, ferry home across the Channel! Thus'. I have omitted the second 'home' on the grounds that it is both tautological and involves an uncharacteristic expansion of the pentameter line.

11-14 An anticipation of 'Anthem for Doomed Youth' (p.12), ll. 9–12:
      What candles may be held to speed them all?
       Not in the hands of boys but in their eyes
      Shall shine the holy glimmers of goodbyes.
      The pallor of girls' brows shall be their pall.

13 Acropole: WO introduces the French word for 'Acropolis', the highest, and usually fortified, part of a Greek city. He was presumably thinking of the Acropolis at Athens, which is built of white marble, but not domed as his image would seem to suggest.

[HAS YOUR SOUL SIPPED]

Has your soul sipped
    Of the sweetness of all sweets?
Has it well supped
    But yet hungers and sweats?

5 I have been witness
    Of a strange sweetness,
All fancy surpassing
    Past all supposing.

Passing the rays
10   Of the rubies of morning,
Or the soft rise
    Of the moon; or the meaning
Known to the rose
    Of her mystery and mourning.

15 Sweeter than nocturnes
    Of the wild nightingale
Or than love's nectar
    After life's gall.

Sweeter than odours
20   Of living leaves,
Sweeter than ardours
    Of dying loves.

Sweeter than death
    And dreams hereafter
25 To one in dearth
    Of life and its laughter.

Or the proud wound
    The victor wears
Or the last end
30   Of all wars.

Or the sweet murder
    After long guard
Unto the martyr
    Smiling at God;

35   To me was that smile,
        Faint as a wan, worn myth
Faint and exceeding small,
    On a boy's murdered mouth.

Though from his throat
40   The life-tide leaps
There was no threat
    On his lips.

But with the bitter blood
    And the death-smell
45   All his life's sweetness bled
    Into a smile.

Written at Craiglockhart in July–August 1917, this would seem to be one of
WO's first experiments in sustained pararhyme. Five of the rhyme words and
'nocturnes' (l. 15) appear in a long list of pararhymes pencilled on the back of a
draft of a fragment, 'The Imbecile' (CP&F, 429), written in Bordeaux in 1913.
On the back of the last MS page of 'Has your soul sipped' WO has written:
'Marlboro' & Other Poems / Chas Sorely'. Sorley's book was published in
January 1916.

CP&F, 232

INSPECTION

'You! What d'you mean by this?' I rapped.
'You dare come on parade like this?'
'Please, sir, it's –' ''Old yer mouth,' the sergeant snapped.
'I takes 'is name, sir?' – 'Please, and then dismiss.'

5   Some days 'confined to camp' he got,
For being 'dirty on parade'.
He told me, afterwards, the damnèd spot
Was blood, his own. 'Well, blood is dirt,' I said.

'Blood's dirt,' he laughed, looking away,
10 Far off to where his wound had bled
And almost merged for ever into clay.
'The world is washing out its stains,' he said.
'It doesn't like our cheeks so red:
Young blood's its great objection.
15 But when we're duly white-washed, being dead,
The race will bear Field Marshal God's inspection.'

Drafted at Craiglockhart in August 1917 and completed in September,
this shows the influence of SS (cp. 'They').

    7 damnèd spot: A reference to *Macbeth*, v.i.35: 'Out, damnèd spot!' This
      'deliberately recalls the occasion of Lady Macbeth's sleepwalking when
      blood was indeed dirt – the irremovable dirt of guilt – and the
      association is sustained a few lines later by the reference to the washing
      out of stains, but the same image also carries a sacrificial overtone ('Are
      you washed in the Blood of the Lamb?') which anticipates the grim irony
      of the final lines' (Welland, 62).

  15 The whitewashing of military installations, kerbstones, etc., was a form
      of superficial cleaning resented by British troops and the target of much
      sarcasm. 'Pipe clay', a form of white clay, is applied with water to whiten
      soldiers' webbing equipment.

CP&F,240

WITH AN IDENTITY DISC

If ever I had dreamed of my dead name
High in the heart of London, unsurpassed
By Time for ever, and the Fugitive, Fame,
There taking a long sanctuary at last,

5   I better that; and recollect with shame
How once I longed to hide it from life's heats
Under those holy cypresses, the same
That keep in shade the quiet place of Keats.

Now, rather, thank I God there is no risk
10 Of gravers scoring it with florid screed,
But let my death be memoried on this disc.
Wear it, sweet friend. Inscribe no date nor deed.
But let thy heart-beat kiss it night and day,
Until the name grow vague and wear away.

Drafted on 23 March 1917, a preliminary fair copy of this sonnet accompanied WO's letter to CO the following day (WO, 175–6). In this he wrote: 'I will send you my last Sonnet, which I started yesterday. I think I will address it to you. *Adieu, mon petit. Je t'embrasse.*' (CL, 446) The poem was revised at Craiglockhart in August–September 1917. It shows the influence of Shakespeare's Sonnet 104, 'To me, fair friend, you never can be old', that in March 1917 WO had copied from memory into the notebook in which he drafted his own, and Keats's sonnet, 'When I have fears that I may cease to be'. Previous editors print an earlier version of ll. 4–8 and emendations proposed by SS to ll. 11 and 14.

    TITLE A British soldier was issued with three identity discs bearing his name and number. They were worn on a cord round his neck and, if he was killed, one was sent to his next of kin.

        2 References to Westminster in the MSS indicate that WO had in mind a memorial in Poets' Corner, Westminster Abbey.

     7–8 Keats is buried among cypress trees in the Protestant Cemetery at Rome.

CP&F, 241

ANTHEM FOR DOOMED YOUTH

What passing-bells for these who die as cattle?
   – Only the monstrous anger of the guns.
   Only the stuttering rifles' rapid rattle
Can patter out their hasty orisons.
5 No mockeries now for them; no prayers nor bells;
   Nor any voice of mourning save the choirs, –
The shrill, demented choirs of wailing shells;
   And bugles calling for them from sad shires.

What candles may be held to speed them all?
10   Not in the hands of boys but in their eyes
Shall shine the holy glimmers of goodbyes.
   The pallor of girls' brows shall be their pall;
Their flowers the tenderness of patient minds,
And each slow dusk a drawing-down of blinds.

Written at Craiglockhart in September–October 1917 (WO, 217–22). SS helped with the revision of the poem and, on 25 September, WO wrote to SO: 'I send you my two best war Poems. Sassoon supplied the title "Anthem": just what I meant it to be.' (CL, 496)

  1 passing-bells: WO was probably responding to the anonymous Prefatory Note to *Poems of Today: an Anthology* (1916), of which he possessed the December 1916 reprint: 'This book has been compiled in order that boys and girls, already perhaps familiar with the great classics of the English speech, may also know something of the newer poetry of their own day. Most of the writers are living, and the rest are still vivid memories among us, while one of the youngest, almost as these words are written, has gone singing to lay down his life for his country's cause ... there is no arbitrary isolation of one theme from another; they mingle and interpenetrate throughout, to the music of Pan's flute, and of Love's viol, and the bugle-call of Endeavour, and the passing-bells of Death.'

  2 Cp. the fragment, 'But I was looking at the permanent stars' (p. 85): 'The monstrous anger of our taciturn guns'.

6–7 Cp. Keats, 'To Autumn', l. 27: 'Then in a wailful choir the small gnats mourn.'

  7 Cp. WO to SO, 2 April 1916: 'The fifers are worthy to rank with the demented violins that make Queen's Hall to spin round as a top, and with the Cathedral Choir that pierces thro' the heights of heaven' (CL, 388).

8 Cp. the fragment. 'I know the music' (p. 84): 'Bugles that sadden all the evening air'; and the fragment, 'But I was looking at the permanent stars' (p.85): 'Bugles sang, saddening the evening air.'

10–11 Cp. Yeats, *Poems* (1895), 'The Wanderings of Oisin', ll. 69: 'A maiden with soft eyes like funeral tapers'.

10–13 Cp. 'A New Heaven' (p. 7), ll. 11–13:
> Weary cathedrals light new shrines for us.
>> To us, rough knees of boys shall ache with rev'rence.
> Are not girls' breasts a clear, strong Acropole?

14 Cp. Laurence Binyon, 'For the Fallen', ll. 15–16: 'At the going down of the sun and in the morning / We will remember them.' DH notes: 'Drawing down the blinds of a house, now an almost forgotten custom, indicated either that a funeral procession was passing or that there had been a death in the house. It was customary to keep the coffin in the house until taking it to church; it would be placed in the darkened parlour, with a pall and flowers on it and lighted candles nearby. Relatives and friends would enter the room to pay their last respects. The sestet of the poem, in fact, refers to a household in mourning.' (DH, 147)

CP&F, 249

SIX O'CLOCK IN PRINCES STREET

In twos and threes, they have not far to roam,
    Crowds that thread eastward, gay of eyes;
Those seek no further than their quiet home,
    Wives, walking westward, slow and wise.

5   Neither should I go fooling over clouds,
    Following gleams unsafe, untrue,
And tiring after beauty through star-crowds,
    Dared I go side by side with you;

Or be you in the gutter where you stand,
    Pale rain-flawed phantom of the place,
With news of all the nations in your hand,
    And all their sorrows in your face.

Written at Craiglockhart some time between August and October 1917 (WO, 124). On 8 August 1917, WO told SO: 'At present I am a sick man in hospital, by night; a poet, for quarter of an hour after breakfast; I am whatever and whoever I see while going down to Edinburgh on the tram: greengrocer, policeman, shopping lady, errand boy, paper-boy, blind man, crippled Tommy, bank-clerk, carter, all of these in half an hour; next a German student in earnest; then I either peer over bookstalls in back-streets, or do a bit of a dash down Princes Street, – according as I have taken weak tea or strong coffee for breakfast' (CL, 480–1).

TITLE Princes Street is one of the main streets of Edinburgh.

4 wives, walking westward: Gillian Nelson calls attention to this and other echoes in the poem of Wordsworth, 'Stepping Westward'.

6 Cp. Tennyson, 'Merlin and the Gleam', ll. 7–10,
    I am Merlin,
    And *I* am dying,
    I am Merlin
    Who follow The Gleam.

WO parodied these lines in his letter of 27 November 1917 to SS: 'I am Owen; and I am dying. / I am Wilfred; and I follow the Gleam' (CL, 512).

7 Cp. Yeats, 'When you are old', l. 12, 'And hid his face amid a crowd of stars.'

10–12 Graham Holliday has pointed out the similarity between these lines and Cowper's description of the postman in *The Task*, iv. 5–7:

[14]

> the herald of a noisy world,
> With spatter'd boots, strapp'd waist, and frozen locks,
> News from all nations lumb'ring at his back.

12 Cp. Yeats, 'When you are old', l. 8, 'And loved the sorrows of your changing face.'

CP&F, 255

1914

War broke: and now the Winter of the world
With perishing great darkness closes in.
The foul tornado, centred at Berlin,
Is over all the width of Europe whirled,
5   Rending the sails of progress. Rent or furled
Are all Art's ensigns. Verse wails. Now begin
Famines of thought and feeling. Love's wine's thin.
The grain of human Autumn rots, down-hurled.

For after Spring had bloomed in early Greece,
10   And Summer blazed her glory out with Rome,
An Autumn softly fell, a harvest home,
A slow grand age, and rich with all increase.
But now, for us, wild Winter, and the need
Of sowings for new Spring, and blood for seed.

Drafted in France in 1914 (WO, 105), and revised either at Craiglockhart in October–November 1917, or at Scarborough between November 1917 and January 1918.

    1 Cp. Shelley, *The Revolt of Islam*, ix. 25: 'This is the winter of the world; – and here/We die.' WO wrote to SO, 18 March 1916: 'Now is the winter of the world. But my life has come already to its month of March.' (CL, 386)

    7 The apparent echo of Rupert Brooke's 'red / Sweet wine of youth' is probably fortuitous. His sonnet 'The Dead' was not published until December 1914, and one draft of '1914' is dated 1914.

    8 Cp. the later MS draft of 'Asleep' (p. 39), l. 18: 'And finished fields of autumns that are old' (MSS, CP&F, 314).

    9 Cp. Keats, 'To Autumn', ll. 23–5:
        Where are the songs of Spring? Aye, where are they?
          Think not of them, thou hast thy music too –
        While barred clouds bloom the soft-dying day.

   12 Cp. Shakespeare, Sonnet 97, l. 6: 'The teeming autumn big with rich increase'.

CP&F, 270

[16]

[I SAW HIS ROUND MOUTH'S CRIMSON]

I saw his round mouth's crimson deepen as it fell,
    Like a sun, in his last deep hour;
Watched the magnificent recession of farewell,
    Clouding, half gleam, half glower,
5 And a last splendour burn the heavens of his cheek.
    And in his eyes
The cold stars lighting, very old and bleak,
    In different skies.

Drafted, probably at Scarborough, in November–December 1917, this poem, or
fragmentary poem, may be a development of the fragment, 'Spells and
Incantation' (p. 87).

    7–8 Cp. Yeats, 'A Dream of Death', l. 9: 'And left her to the indifferent stars
      above.'

CP&F, 277

APOLOGIA PRO POEMATE MEO

I, too, saw God through mud, –
    The mud that cracked on cheeks when wretches smiled.
    War brought more glory to their eyes than blood,
    And gave their laughs more glee than shakes a child.

5 Merry it was to laugh there –
    Where death becomes absurd and life absurder.
    For power was on us as we slashed bones bare
    Not to feel sickness or remorse of murder.

I, too, have dropped off Fear –
10   Behind the barrage, dead as my platoon,
    And sailed my spirit surging light and clear
    Past the entanglement where hopes lay strewn;

And witnessed exultation –
    Faces that used to curse me, scowl for scowl,
15   Shine and lift up with passion of oblation,
    Seraphic for an hour; though they were foul.

I have made fellowships –
    Untold of happy lovers in old song.
    For love is not the binding of fair lips
20   With the soft silk of eyes that look and long,

By Joy, whose ribbon slips, –
    But wound with war's hard wire whose stakes are strong;
    Bound with the bandage of the arm that drips;
    Knit in the webbing of the rifle-thong.

25 I have perceived much beauty
    In the hoarse oaths that kept our courage straight;
    Heard music in the silentness of duty;
    Found peace where shell-storms spouted reddest spate.

Nevertheless, except you share
30   With them in hell the sorrowful dark of hell,
    Whose world is but the trembling of a flare
    And heaven but as the highway for a shell,

You shall not hear their mirth:
  You shall not come to think them well content
35   By any jest of mine. These men are worth
  Your tears. You are not worth their merriment.

Written at Scarborough in November–December 1917 (WO, 250–2). The final
fair copy is dated 'Nov. 1917', but it is tempting to see the poem as a response to
a remark in Robert Graves's letter *c.* 22 December 1917: 'For God's sake
cheer up and write more optimistically – The war's not ended yet but a poet
should have a spirit above wars' (CL, 596). Graves may have said much the same
to WO earlier.

TITLE SS corrected the faulty Latin grammar of WO's own title, 'Apologia pro
    Poema Mea', which may have been influenced by that of Cardinal
    Newman's *Apologia Pro Vita Sua.*

And have we done with War at last?
Well, we've been lucky devils both,
And there's no need of pledge or oath
To bind our lovely friendship fast,
By firmer stuff
Close bound enough.

By wire and wood and stake we're bound,
By Fricourt and by Festubert,
By whipping rain, by the sun's glare,

By all the misery and loud sound,
By a Spring day,
By a Picard clay.

Show me the two so closely bound,
As we, by the wet bond of blood,
By friendship, blossoming from mud,
By Death: we faced him, and we found
Beauty in Death,
In dead men breath.

  1 too: Welland, 67–8, argues convincingly that this is an allusion to
    Graves's poem 'Two Fusiliers':

 13 exultation: Cp. Shelley, 'A Defence of Poetry': 'Poetry is a mirror which
    makes beautiful that which is distorted . . . it exalts the beauty of that
    which is most beautiful, and it adds beauty to that which is most
    deformed; it marries exultation and horror.'

18–20 Cp. ELG, 'L'Amour', published in *The Nymph and Other Poems*
    (November 1917), ll. 1–2: 'Love is the binding of souls together, / The
    binding of lips, the binding of eyes.'

 21 Cp. Keats, 'Ode on Melancholy', l. 22: 'And Joy, whose hand is ever at
    his lips'.

CP&F, 278

LE CHRISTIANISME

So the church Christ was hit and buried
  Under its rubbish and its rubble.
In cellars, packed-up saints lie serried,
  Well out of hearing of our trouble.

5 One Virgin still immaculate
    Smiles on for war to flatter her.
She's halo'd with an old tin hat,
    But a piece of hell will batter her.

Written, probably at Scarborough, in late November or early December 1917.
At the foot of the corrected fair copy WO has written 'Quivières', a village
where he was quartered in April 1917 (WO, 183), but as Quivières has no church,
his memory may have been at fault.

    1 Cp. 'At a Calvary near the Ancre' (p. 23), ll. 1–2.

    4 Cp. A. E. Housman, 'On Wenlock edge the wood's in trouble', ll. 19–20:
      'Today the Roman and his trouble / Are ashes under Uricon.'

    8 A pun may be intended, 'piece' meaning both fragment and field-gun,
      as opposed to 'the peace of God'.

CP&F, 281

[20]

HOSPITAL BARGE

Budging the sluggard ripples of the Somme,
A barge round old Cérisy slowly slewed.
Softly her engines down the current screwed,
And chuckled softly with contented hum,
5   Till fairy tinklings struck their croonings dumb.
The waters rumpling at the stern subdued;
The lock-gate took her bulging amplitude;
Gently from out the gurgling lock she swum.

One reading by that calm bank shaded eyes
10 To watch her lessening westward quietly.
Then, as she neared the bend, her funnel screamed.
And that long lamentation made him wise
How unto Avalon, in agony,
Kings passed in the dark barge which Merlin dreamed.

Written at Scarborough in December 1917, following 'a Saturday night revel in
"The Passing of Arthur" ' (EB, 124; see also WO, 248–9). On 10 May 1917, WO
had written to SO: 'I sailed in a steam-tug about 6 miles down the Canal with
another "inmate". The heat of the afternoon was Augustan; and it has probably
added another year to my old age to have been able to escape marching in
equipment under such a sun. The scenery was such as I never saw or dreamed
of since I read the *Fairie Queene*. Just as in the Winter when I woke up lying on
the burning cold snow I fancied I must have died & been pitch-forked into the
Wrong Place, so, yesterday, it was not more difficult to imagine that my dusky
barge was wending up to Avalon, and the peace of Arthur, and where Lancelot
heals him of his grievous wound. But the Saxon is not broken, as we could very
well hear last night. Later, a real thunderstorm did its best to seem terrible, and
quite failed.' (CL, 457)

   2 Cérisy is one and a half miles down the Somme Canal from Gailly where
      WO was a patient in the 13th Casualty Clearing Station.

   9 reading: The poem implies that the speaker was reading Malory, *Le
      Morte Darthur*, or a later retelling such as Tennyson, 'The Passing of
      Arthur', from *The Holy Grail and Other Poems* (1870). WO bought a copy
      of the latter book in Edinburgh in July 1917.

   12 lamentation: Cp. Tennyson, 'The Passing of Arthur', ll. 361–71:
          Then saw they how there hove a dusky barge,
       Dark as a funeral scarf from stem to stern,

Beneath them; and descending they were ware
That all the decks were dense with stately forms,
Black-stoled, black-hooded, like a dream – by these
Three Queens with crowns of gold: and from them rose
A cry that shivered to the tingling stars,
And, as it were one voice, an agony
Of lamentation, like a wind that shrills
All night in a waste land, where no one comes
Or hath come, since the making of the world.

14 In November 1917 WO had marked in his copy of Alfred Austin, *Songs
of England* (1898), 'The Passing of Merlin', v:
A wailing cometh from the shores that veil
Avilion's island valley; on the mere,
Looms through the mist and wet winds weeping blear
A dusky barge, which, without oar or sail,
Fades to the far-off fields where falls nor snow nor hail.

CP&F, 281

AT A CALVARY NEAR THE ANCRE

One ever hangs where shelled roads part.
　　In this war He too lost a limb,
But His disciples hide apart;
　　And now the Soldiers bear with Him.

5　Near Golgotha strolls many a priest,
　　And in their faces there is pride
That they were flesh-marked by the Beast
　　By whom the gentle Christ's denied.

The scribes on all the people shove
10　　And bawl allegiance to the state,
But they who love the greater love
　　Lay down their life; they do not hate.

Written probably in late 1917 or early 1918, WO having been involved in
fighting near the river Ancre in January 1917 (CL., 421 n.). DH's note is to the
point: 'As in "The Parable of the Old Man and the Young", WO adapts
Biblical detail to fit the war. In the Gospel story, the *Soldiers* kept watch at
the cross while Christ's *disciples* hid in fear of the authorities; *priests* and *scribes*
passed by in scorn. The Church sends priests to the trenches, where they watch
the common soldier being, as it were, crucified, and they take pride in minor
wounds (*flesh-marked*, l. 7) as a sign of their opposition to Germany (*the Beast*).
Flesh-marked, however, carries a further meaning: the Devil used to be believed
to leave his finger-marks on the flesh of his followers (cf. Revelation 14:9–10).
Thus the Church's hatred of Germany (l. 12) puts it in the Devil's following;
and the priests' wounds are signs not so much of opposition to the Devil
Germany as of allegiance to the Devil War. Christ said "Love one another" *and*
"Love your enemies"; despite the exhortations of Church and State, WO
perceives that "pure Christianity will not fit in with pure patriotism" [CL., 461].'
(DH, 116)

TITLE　Calvary or Golgotha (both words meaning 'the place of the skull', from
　　　　Lat. *calvaria* and Heb. *gulgōleth* respectively) was the site of the
　　　　Crucifixion. A Calvary is a model of the crucified Christ, such as is
　　　　found at many crossroads in France.

　　4　Two senses of 'bear with' seem intended: 'humour' and 'carry the cross
　　　　with'.

11–12　John 15: 13: 'Greater love hath no man than this, that a man lay down
　　　　his life for his friends.' See also 'Greater Love' (p.53).

CP&F, 287

MINERS

There was a whispering in my hearth,
    A sigh of the coal,
Grown wistful of a former earth
    It might recall.

5 I listened for a tale of leaves
    And smothered ferns,
Frond-forests, and the low sly lives
    Before the fawns.

My fire might show steam-phantoms simmer
10   From Time's old cauldron,
Before the birds made nests in summer,
    Or men had children.

But the coals were murmuring of their mine,
    And moans down there
15 Of boys that slept wry sleep, and men
    Writhing for air.

And I saw white bones in the cinder-shard,
    Bones without number.
Many the muscled bodies charred,
20   And few remember.

I thought of all that worked dark pits
    Of war, and died
Digging the rock where Death reputes
    Peace lies indeed.

25 Comforted years will sit soft-chaired,
    In rooms of amber;
The years will stretch their hands, well-cheered
    By our life's ember;

The centuries will burn rich loads
30   With which we groaned,
Whose warmth shall lull their dreaming lids,

While songs are crooned;
But they will not dream of us poor lads,
    Left in the ground.

Written at Scarborough on 13 or 14 January 1918 (WO, 253–7). On 12 January a
pit explosion at the Podmore Hall Colliery, Halmerend, killed about 140 men
and boy miners. WO presumably read the newspaper accounts, that in the *Daily
News* of 14 January being headlined 'Colliery Disaster', and the same day he told
SO: 'Wrote a poem on the Colliery Disaster: but I get mixed up with the War at
the end. It is short, but oh! sour.' (EB, 125). He showed it to SS, who proposed
alterations which, with questionable judgement, WO would seem to have
accepted (see CP&F, 287). On 17 January he sent his mother 'the Coal Poem'
and two days later wrote to her: 'With your beautiful letter came a proof from the
Nation of my "Miners". This is the first poem I have sent to the *Nation* myself,
and it has evidently been accepted. It was scrawled out on the back of a note to
the Editor; and no penny stamp or addressed envelope was enclosed for return!
That's the way to do it. "Miners" will probably appear next Saturday [26
January].' It did, and that evening WO wrote to ELG: 'You may feel keen
enough to buy this week's *Nation*. I have at last a poem in it, which I sent off on
the same evening as writing!!.' This produced 'blunt criticism' from ELG,
whose 'musical ear' was offended by his cousin's rhymes, and on 12 February
WO replied: 'I suppose I am doing in poetry what the advanced composers are
doing in music. I am not satisfied with either. Still I am satisfied with the Two
Guineas that half-hour's work brought me. Got the Cheque this m'ng!'
(CL, 527–31)

   DH ('Wilfred Owen and the Georgians', RES, n.s., xxx, no. 117 (1979), 28–40)
has detected the influence of the introductory poem in W. W. Gibson's *Fires*
(1912). Gibson sees pleasant pictures in the embers, including forests:
    Till, dazzled by the drowsy glare,
    I shut my eyes to heat and light;
    And saw, in sudden night,
    Crouched in the dripping dark,
    With steaming shoulders stark,
    The man who hews the coal to feed my fire.
In 'Miners', the watcher by the hearth expects the coal to tell of its prehistoric
origin – WO was an amateur geologist – but instead it speaks of the sufferings
of miners, in whom WO had been interested (WO, 76–8, 136–7, 230) long
before he commanded a platoon containing several in 1916. The Halmerend
disaster prompts a vision of the fate of such miners and those others who dug
perilous 'saps' under No Man's Land to mine the enemy lines. At the poem's
end WO sees himself sharing their common trench, mine, grave, hell. See
Jennifer Breen, 'The Dating and Sources of Wilfred Owen's "Miners"', N&Q,
n.s., xxi, no. 10 (October 1974), 366–70, and William Cooke, 'Wilfred Owen's
"Miners" and the Minnie Pit Disaster', *English*, xxvi, no. 126 (Autumn 1977),
213–17.

   8 fawns: Cp. 'Sweet is your antique body, not yet young' (JS, 106), l.8.

THE LETTER

With B.E.F. June 10. Dear Wife,
(Oh blast this pencil. 'Ere, Bill, lend's a knife.)
I'm in the pink at present, dear.
I think the war will end this year.
5   We don't see much of them square-'eaded 'Uns.
We're out of harm's way, not bad fed.
I'm longing for a taste of your old buns.
(Say, Jimmie, spare's a bite of bread.)
There don't seem much to say just now.
10   (Yer what? Then don't, yer ruddy cow!
And give us back me cigarette!)
I'll soon be 'ome. You mustn't fret.
My feet's improvin', as I told you of.
We're out in rest now. Never fear.
15   (VRACH! By crumbs, but that was near.)
Mother might spare you half a sov.
Kiss Neil and Bert. When me and you –
(Eh? What the 'ell! Stand to? Stand to!
Jim, give's a hand with pack on, lad.
20   Guh! Christ! I'm hit. Take 'old. Aye, bad.
No, damn your iodine. Jim? 'Ere!
Write my old girl, Jim, there's a dear.)

Written, probably at Scarborough but possibly at Ripon, between January and
March 1918.
  1   B.E.F.: British Expeditionary Force.
  3   in the pink: in very good health.
  18 Stand to: Abbreviated form of the command 'Stand to arms', meaning
       'Prepare for/to attack'.

CP&F, 288

---

  19 Previous editors read 'For many hearts with coal are charred', an
       interlinear suggestion added to the MS by SS. I prefer WO's original
       line.
  24 lies: A pun would be in keeping with the tone of the poem.
  34 Previous editors read 'Lost in the ground', an interlinear suggestion
       added to the MS by SS. I prefer WO's original verb.

CP&F, 287

CONSCIOUS

His fingers wake, and flutter; up the bed.
His eyes come open with a pull of will,
Helped by the yellow mayflowers by his head.
The blind-cord drawls across the window-sill . . .
5 What a smooth floor the ward has! What a rug!
Who is that talking somewhere out of sight?
Three flies are creeping round the shiny jug . . .
'Nurse! Doctor!' – 'Yes, all right, all right.'

But sudden evening blurs and fogs the air.
10 There seems no time to want a drink of water.
Nurse looks so far away. And here and there
Music and roses burst through crimson slaughter.
He can't remember where he saw blue sky . . .
The trench is narrower. Cold, he's cold; yet hot –
15 And there's no light to see the voices by . . .
There is no time to ask . . . he knows not what.

Written, probably at Scarborough but possibly at Ripon, between January and
March 1918, this poem shows the influence of SS, 'The Death-Bed' (WO, 256).

  3 Cp. WO to MO from 13th Casualty Clearing Station, 8 May 1917:
     'Meanwhile I have superb weather, sociably-possible friends, great blue
     bowls of yellow Mayflower, baths and bed *ad lib*' (CL, 456).

  9 Cp. WO to SO, 14 August 1912: 'sudden twilight seemed to fall upon
     the world' (CL, 153).

  10 Cp. SS, 'The Death-Bed', l. 7: 'Someone was holding water to his
     mouth.'

  12 Cp. SS, 'The Death-Bed', l. 9: 'Through crimson gloom to darkness'.

CP&F, 288

SCHOOLMISTRESS

Having, with bold Horatius, stamped her feet
And waved a final swashing arabesque
O'er the brave days of old, she ceased to bleat,
Slapped her Macaulay back upon the desk,
5   Resumed her calm gaze and her lofty seat.

There, while she heard the classic lines repeat,
Once more the teacher's face clenched stern;
For through the window, looking on the street,
Three soldiers hailed her. She made no return.
10 One was called 'Orace whom she would not greet.

Written, probably at Scarborough but possibly at Ripon, between January and March 1918, this poem may derive from WO's experience at the Tynecastle Secondary School, Edinburgh, where he gave English lessons in September–October 1917 (WO, 215).

TITLE EB and CDL entitle this poem 'Bold Horatius'.

   1 The schoolmistress has been reading Thomas Babington Macaulay's poem 'Horatius' from *Lays of Ancient Rome*.

CP&F, 290

DULCE ET DECORUM EST

Bent double, like old beggars under sacks,
Knock-kneed, coughing like hags, we cursed through sludge,
Till on the haunting flares we turned our backs
And towards our distant rest began to trudge.
5 Men marched asleep. Many had lost their boots
But limped on, blood-shod. All went lame; all blind;
Drunk with fatigue; deaf even to the hoots
Of tired, outstripped Five-Nines that dropped behind.

Gas! GAS! Quick, boys! – An ecstasy of fumbling,
10 Fitting the clumsy helmets just in time;
But someone still was yelling out and stumbling,
And flound'ring like a man in fire or lime . . .
Dim, through the misty panes and thick green light,
As under a green sea, I saw him drowning.

15 In all my dreams, before my helpless sight,
He plunges at me, guttering, choking, drowning.

If in some smothering dreams you too could pace
Behind the wagon that we flung him in,
And watch the white eyes writhing in his face,
20 His hanging face, like a devil's sick of sin;
If you could hear, at every jolt, the blood
Come gargling from the froth-corrupted lungs,
Obscene as cancer, bitter as the cud
Of vile, incurable sores on innocent tongues, –
25 My friend, you would not tell with such high zest
To children ardent for some desperate glory,
The old Lie: Dulce et decorum est
Pro patria mori.

Drafted at Craiglockhart in the first half of October 1917 (WO, 226–8), this poem
was revised, probably at Scarborough but possibly at Ripon, between January
and March 1918. The earliest surviving MS is dated 'Oct. 8. 1917', and on the
[? 16th] WO wrote to SO: 'Here is a gas poem, done yesterday, (which is not
private, but not final). The famous Latin tag [from Horace, *Odes*, III. ii. 13]

means of course <u>It is sweet and meet to die for one's country</u>. <u>Sweet</u>! and <u>decorous</u>!' (CL, 499–500)

5 Men . . . Many: Cp. WO to SO, 16 January 1917: '. . . craters full of water. Men have been known to drown in them. Many stuck in the mud . . .' (CL, 427)

8 WO never finalized this line (see MS on CP&F, 292). Five-Nines: 5.9-calibre shells.

9 GAS: Cp. WO to SO, 19 January 1917: 'I went on ahead to scout – foolishly alone – and when, half a mile away from the party, got overtaken by GAS' (CL, 428).

12 flound'ring: 'I remember [WO] using this word floundering and, unable to resist the play, adding, " . . . but of course, there is, I suppose, the possibility you might founder" ' (JFO, III. 132).

13 panes: The gas mask's celluloid windows.

17-25 you . . . My friend: Jessie Pope, to whom the poem was originally to have been dedicated, was the author of numerous pre-war children's books, as well as of *Jessie Pope's War Poems* (1915), *More War Poems* (1915), and *Simple Rhymes for Stirring Times* (1916) (WO, 227).

CP&F, 292

THE DEAD-BEAT

He dropped, – more sullenly than wearily,
Lay stupid like a cod, heavy like meat,
And none of us could kick him to his feet;
– Just blinked at my revolver, blearily;
5   – Didn't appear to know a war was on,
Or see the blasted trench at which he stared.
'I'll do 'em in,' he whined. 'If this hand's spared,
I'll murder them, I will.'

                A low voice said,
'It's Blighty, p'raps, he sees; his pluck's all gone,
10 Dreaming of all the valiant, that *aren't* dead:
Bold uncles, smiling ministerially;
Maybe his brave young wife, getting her fun
In some new home, improved materially.
It's not these stiffs have crazed him; nor the Hun.'

15 We sent him down at last, out of the way.
Unwounded; – stout lad, too, before that strafe.
Malingering? Stretcher-bearers winked, 'Not half!'

Next day I heard the Doc's well-whiskied laugh:
'That scum you sent last night soon died. Hooray!'

Begun on 22 August 1917, when WO wrote to ELG: 'At last I have an event worth a letter. I have beknown myself to Siegfried Sassoon. Went in to him last night (my second call) . . . After leaving him, I wrote something in Sassoon's style, which I may as well send you, since you ask for the latest.' A fair copy of 'The Dead-Beat' followed, and the next day WO continued his letter: '. . . He was struck with the "Dead Beat", but pointed out that the facetious bit was out of keeping with the first & last stanzas. Thus the piece as a whole is no good.' (CL, 485–6) WO salvaged – and probably adapted – eight lines of 'the facetious bit' for his editorial in *The Hydra*, no. 10 (1 September 1917). The poem was revised at Ripon between March and May 1918.

    9 Blighty: soldiers' slang for 'Britain'.
   16 strafe: artillery bombardment (from the German phrase, *Gott strafe England*, meaning 'God punish England').

CP&F, 298

INSENSIBILITY

1

Happy are men who yet before they are killed
Can let their veins run cold.
Whom no compassion fleers
Or makes their feet
5   Sore on the alleys cobbled with their brothers.
The front line withers.
But they are troops who fade, not flowers,
For poets' tearful fooling:
Men, gaps for filling:
10 Losses, who might have fought
Longer; but no one bothers.

2

And some cease feeling
Even themselves or for themselves.
Dullness best solves
15 The tease and doubt of shelling,
And Chance's strange arithmetic
Comes simpler than the reckoning of their shilling.
They keep no check on armies' decimation.

3

Happy are these who lose imagination:
20 They have enough to carry with ammunition.
Their spirit drags no pack.
Their old wounds, save with cold, can not more ache.
Having seen all things red,
Their eyes are rid
25 Of the hurt of the colour of blood for ever.
And terror's first constriction over,
Their hearts remain small-drawn.
Their senses in some scorching cautery of battle
Now long since ironed,
30 Can laugh among the dying, unconcerned.

4

Happy the soldier home, with not a notion
How somewhere, every dawn, some men attack,
And many sighs are drained.
Happy the lad whose mind was never trained:
His days are worth forgetting more than not.
He sings along the march
Which we march taciturn, because of dusk,
The long, forlorn, relentless trend
From larger day to huger night.

5

We wise, who with a thought besmirch
Blood over all our soul,
How should we see our task
But through his blunt and lashless eyes?
Alive, he is not vital overmuch;
Dying, not mortal overmuch;
Nor sad, nor proud,
Nor curious at all.
He cannot tell
Old men's placidity from his.

6

But cursed are dullards whom no cannon stuns,
That they should be as stones.
Wretched are they, and mean
With paucity that never was simplicity.
By choice they made themselves immune
To pity and whatever moans in man
Before the last sea and the hapless stars;
Whatever mourns when many leave these shores;
Whatever shares
The eternal reciprocity of tears.

Drafted either at Craiglockhart in October–November 1917, or at Scarborough between November 1917 and January 1918, this Pindaric ode – perhaps a reply to Wordsworth's 'Character of the Happy Warrior' (WO, 261) – may have been revised at Ripon in April 1918. WO wrote to ELG on 21 April: 'In my

Chaumbers under the roof of a cottage (7 Borage Lane, Ripon) I have written, I think, two poems: one an Ode which, considering my tuneless tendencies, may be called dam good, excuse me' (CL, 546–7). However, DH argues persuasively (in a letter to the editor) that WO is here referring to his 'Elegy in April and September' (p. 70), which in its April version was entitled 'Ode for a Poet' and given musical annotations.

TITLE   Cp. Shelley, 'A Defence of Poetry': 'It [Poetry] is as it were the interpenetration of a diviner nature through our own; but its footsteps are like those of a wind over a sea, which the coming calm erases, and those traces remain only, as on the wrinkled sand which paves it. These and corresponding conditions of being are experienced principally by those of the most delicate sensibility and the most enlarged imagination; and the state of mind produced by them is at war with every base desire.'

1   Cp. Wordsworth, 'Character of the Happy Warrior', ll. 1–2: 'Who is the happy Warrior? Who is he / That every man in arms should wish to be?'

5   cobbled with their brothers: Cp. WO to MO, ?25 March 1918: 'They are dying again at Beaumont Hamel, which already in 1916 was cobbled with skulls' (CL, 542).

8   fooling: Cp. 'Six O'clock in Princes Street' (p. 14), l. 5: 'Neither should I go fooling over clouds.'

9   gaps for filling: DH notes that 'The gaps had been illustrated on a number of recruiting posters. "Fill up the Ranks!" was a familiar slogan; one poster shows a long line of men in which a single empty space is filled by a billboard marked "This space is Reserved for a Fit Man". The repeated use of the word "happy" in the . . . poem, to describe the soldier who has been rendered "insensible to war" by war experience, is reminiscent of another poster which shows a smiling Tommy and the caption, "He's happy and satisfied / Are You?".' ('Some Contemporary Allusions in Poems by Rosenberg, Owen and Sassoon', N&Q, n.s., xxvi, no. 4 [August 1979], 333)

17   shilling: The 'King's shilling' was that traditionally given to the newly enlisted soldier by the recruiting officer.

19   imagination: Cp. Shelley, 'A Defence of Poetry', quoted above.

40   We wise: we poets.

55   moans: SS, CDL, and DH (but see DH, 125) read 'mourns'. WO, however, clearly cancelled 'mourns' and wrote 'moans' above it. See CP&F, p. 301.

56   Cp. Tennyson, 'Oenone', l. 215: 'Between the loud stream and the trembling stars'.

59   reciprocity: Cp. John Drinkwater, 'Reciprocity', a poem printed in *The Hydra*, New Series, no. 1, 2. There is a MS among WO's papers.

CP&F, 301

[34]

STRANGE MEETING

It seemed that out of battle I escaped
Down some profound dull tunnel, long since scooped
Through granites which titanic wars had groined.

Yet also there encumbered sleepers groaned,
5   Too fast in thought or death to be bestirred.
Then, as I probed them, one sprang up, and stared
With piteous recognition in fixed eyes,
Lifting distressful hands, as if to bless.
And by his smile, I knew that sullen hall, –
10   By his dead smile I knew we stood in Hell.

With a thousand pains that vision's face was grained;
Yet no blood reached there from the upper ground,
And no guns thumped, or down the flues made moan.
'Strange friend,' I said, 'here is no cause to mourn.'
15   'None,' said that other, 'save the undone years,
The hopelessness. Whatever hope is yours,
Was my life also; I went hunting wild
After the wildest beauty in the world,
Which lies not calm in eyes, or braided hair,
20   But mocks the steady running of the hour,
And if it grieves, grieves richlier than here.
For by my glee might many men have laughed,
And of my weeping something had been left,
Which must die now. I mean the truth untold,
25   The pity of war, the pity war distilled.
Now men will go content with what we spoiled,
Or, discontent, boil bloody, and be spilled.
They will be swift with swiftness of the tigress.
None will break ranks, though nations trek from progress.
30   Courage was mine, and I had mystery,
Wisdom was mine, and I had mastery:
To miss the march of this retreating world
Into vain citadels that are not walled.
Then, when much blood had clogged their chariot-wheels,
35   I would go up and wash them from sweet wells,
Even with truths that lie too deep for taint.

I would have poured my spirit without stint
But not through wounds; not on the cess of war.
Foreheads of men have bled where no wounds were.

40 'I am the enemy you killed, my friend.
I knew you in this dark: for so you frowned
Yesterday through me as you jabbed and killed.
I parried; but my hands were loath and cold.
Let us sleep now . . . .'

Drafted, probably at Scarborough but possibly at Ripon, between January
and March 1918, this poem may be a development of the fragment, 'With
those that are become' (CP&F, 492), drafted in November 1917. Certainly, it
incorporates another fragment, 'Earth's wheels run oiled with blood' (CP&F, 514),
written between November 1917 and January 1918. For a full and illuminating
discussion of the interplay of echoes in 'Strange Meeting' from the Bible,
Barbusse, Cary's translation of Dante, Keats, Shelley, Sir Lewis Morris,
Harold Munro, and SS, see Bäckman, 96–117. The MSS suggests that WO
may not have regarded the poem as complete.

TITLE Welland was the first to cp. Shelley, *The Revolt of Islam*, ll. 1828–32:
        And one whose spear had pierced me, leaned beside,
            With quivering lips and humid eyes; – and all
        Seemed like some brothers on a journey wide
            Gone forth, whom now strange meeting did befall
        In a strange land . . .
    Cp. also Harold Munro, *Strange Meetings* (1917).

2 tunnel: cp. SS, 'The Rear-Guard', ll. 1–3:
        Groping along the tunnel, step by step,
        He winked his prying torch with patching glare
        From side to side, and sniffed the unwholesome air.
    Bäckman suggests the influence of a childhood memory of a nightmare
    walk down an 'immensely long and dark' drive, roofed with trees 'so that
    the effect was of a rather dark tunnel' (JFO, 1. 80).
    scooped: Cp. Shelley, *The Revolt of Islam*, ll. 2913–15:
        He plunged through the green silence of the main,
            Through many a cavern which the eternal flood
            Had scooped, as dark lairs for its monster brood . . .
    Also *Alastor*, ll. 423–5:
                                        There, huge caves,
        Scooped in the dark base of their aëry rocks
        Mocking its moans, respond and roar for ever.

3 granites: Cp. WO to SO, 18? February 1917: 'the men had to dig
    trenches in ground like granite' (CL., 436).

4 encumbered: Cp, WO to SO, 1 February 1916: 'When I was going up the subway at Liverpool St. from the Underground to the Gt. Eastern Platform, I noticed the passages unduly encumbered, and found the outlet just closed' (CL, 377).

6–11 Cp. the poet's vision of Moneta's face, 'bright-blanched / By an immortal sickness which kills not' in Keats, 'The Fall of Hyperion'; also Dante, *Hell* (in the 1805 translation by the Revd. Henry Francis Cary, a copy of which WO possessed), XV. 22–9:
> I was agnized of one, who by the skirt
> Caught me, and cried, What wonder have we here?'
> And I, when he to me outstretch'd his arm,
>   Intently fix'd my ken on his parch'd looks,
> That, although smirch'd with fire, they hinder'd not
> But I remember'd him; and towards his face
>   My hand inclining, answered, 'Ser Brunetto!
> And are ye here?'

25 Cp. WO's Preface (p. 98): 'My subject is War, and the pity of War. The Poetry is in the pity.'

28 Cp. II Samuel 1:23: 'Saul and Jonathan were lovely and pleasant in their lives, and in their death they were not divided: they were swifter than eagles, they were stronger than lions.'

29 Presumably an allusion to the Great Trek of the South African Boer farmers in 1835–6.

32 Cp. 'The Fates' (JS, 64), l. 14: 'And miss the march of lifetime, stage by stage.'

34 chariot-wheels: Cp. Shelley, *Queen Mab*, VII. 33–5:
>   whether hosts
> Stain his death-blushing chariot-wheels, as on
> Triumphantly they roll, . . .

36 Cp. Wordsworth, Ode on 'Intimations of Immortality from Recollections of Early Childhood', l. 205: 'Thoughts that do often lie too deep for tears'.

39 Cp. Luke 22:44: 'and his sweat was as it were great drops of blood falling to the ground.'

40 Cp. Oscar Wilde, 'The Ballad of Reading Gaol', l. 37: 'Yet each man kills the thing he loves.' This line, misquoted, appears in the fragment, 'With those that are become' (CP&F, 492). Cp. also Henri Barbusse, *Under Fire* (1917), 288: 'When I'm sleeping I dream that I'm killing him over again!'

44 Cp. 'Science has looked and sees no life but this' (JS, 15): 'Let me but sleep . . .', and the fragment, 'The Women and the Slain' (CP&F, 502): 'Keep silent. Let us sleep' (line cancelled).

CP&F, 306

SONNET

On Seeing a Piece of Our Heavy Artillery
Brought into Action

Be slowly lifted up, thou long black arm,
Great Gun towering towards Heaven, about to curse;
Sway steep against them, and for years rehearse
Huge imprecations like a blasting charm!
5   Reach at that Arrogance which needs thy harm,
And beat it down before its sins grow worse.
Spend our resentment, cannon, – yea, disburse
Our gold in shapes of flame, our breaths in storm.

Yet, for men's sakes whom thy vast malison
10 Must wither innocent of enmity,
Be not withdrawn, dark arm, thy spoilure done,
Safe to the bosom of our prosperity.
But when thy spell be cast complete and whole,
May God curse thee, and cut thee from our soul!

Revised at Scarborough in May 1918, but perhaps begun as early as July 1917.

9 malison: malediction, curse.

CP&F, 311

[38]

ASLEEP

Under his helmet, up against his pack,
After so many days of work and waking,
Sleep took him by the brow and laid him back.

There, in the happy no-time of his sleeping,
5   Death took him by the heart. There heaved a quaking
Of the aborted life within him leaping,
Then chest and sleepy arms once more fell slack.

And soon the slow, stray blood came creeping
From the intruding lead, like ants on track.

10   Whether his deeper sleep lie shaded by the shaking
Of great wings, and the thoughts that hung the stars,
High-pillowed on calm pillows of God's making,
Above these clouds, these rains, these sleets of lead,
And these winds' scimitars,
15   - Or whether yet his thin and sodden head
Confuses more and more with the low mould,
His hair being one with the grey grass
Of finished fields, and wire-scrags rusty-old,
Who knows? Who hopes? Who troubles? Let it pass!
20   He sleeps. He sleeps less tremulous, less cold,
Than we who wake, and waking say Alas!

Written, probably in Shrewsbury, on 14 November 1917 (wo, 237–8) and
revised at Ripon the following May. On 16 November 1917, WO wrote to ELG:
'Good of you to send me the Lyric of Nov. 14th. I can only send my own of the
same date, which came from Winchester Downs, as I crossed the long backs of
the downs after leaving you. It is written as from the trenches. I could almost see
the dead lying about in the hollows of the downs.' (cl, 508) The subject of the
poem suggests an acquaintance with Rimbaud's 'Le dormeur du val'. DH
argues persuasively for the influence of Robert Graves's *Fairies and Fusiliers*
(1917), which WO bought on the day he began 'Asleep' ('Wilfred Owen and the

Georgians', RES, n.s., xxx, no. 117 (1979), 36); and Bäckman detects and discusses (40–2) an important debt to Milton's 'Lycidas'. Previous editors follow an earlier version.

1–9 Cp. Swinburne, 'Laus Veneris', ll. 1–4:
     Asleep or waking is it? for her neck,
     Kissed over close, wears yet a purple speck
       Wherein the pained blood falters and goes out;
     Soft, and stung softly – fairer for a fleck.

17 Cp. WO to SO, 24 May 1914: 'It was curious you asked about my grey hairs, for just last week I noticed they were cropping up again. In winter they died down, with the grass.' (CL, 252)

CP&F, 312

ARMS AND THE BOY

Let the boy try along this bayonet-blade
How cold steel is, and keen with hunger of blood;
Blue with all malice, like a madman's flash;
And thinly drawn with famishing for flesh.

5   Lend him to stroke these blind, blunt bullet-leads,
Which long to nuzzle in the hearts of lads,
Or give him cartridges whose fine zinc teeth
Are sharp with sharpness of grief and death.

For his teeth seem for laughing round an apple.
10 There lurk no claws behind his fingers supple;
And God will grow no talons at his heels,
Nor antlers through the thickness of his curls.

Written, or at any rate fair-copied, at 7 Borrage Lane, Ripon, on 3 May 1918, this poem was classified by WO in his draft list of contents (CP&F, 539) under 'Protest – the unnaturalness of weapons'.

TITLE Cp. SS, 'Arms and the Man' and Harold Monro, 'Youth in Arms'.

1–4 Cp.Shelley, *The Mask of Anarchy*, lxxvii. ll. 311–14:
>Let the fixèd bayonet
>Gleam with sharp desire to wet
>Its bright point in English blood
>Looking keen as one for food.

6 Paul Fussell observes that 'Bret Harte's "What the Bullet Sang", one of the few American poems available in the *Oxford Book [of English Verse,* edited by Sir Arthur Quiller-Couch]*, seems to lie behind both Sassoon's "The Kiss" and Owen's "Arms and the Boy", both of which, like Harte's poem, make much of the quasi-erotic desire of the bullet (and in Sassoon, the bayonet) to "kiss" or "nuzzle" the body of its adolescent target.' (*The Great War and Modern Memory* [1975], 160)

CP&F, 315

THE SHOW

> We have fallen in the dreams the ever-living
> Breathe on the tarnished mirror of the world,
> And then smooth out with ivory hands and sigh.
> W. B. YEATS

My soul looked down from a vague height, with Death,
As unremembering how I rose or why,
And saw a sad land, weak with sweats of dearth,
Grey, cratered like the moon with hollow woe,
5 And pitted with great pocks and scabs of plagues.

Across its beard, that horror of harsh wire,
There moved thin caterpillars, slowly uncoiled.
It seemed they pushed themselves to be as plugs
Of ditches, where they writhed and shrivelled, killed.

10 By them had slimy paths been trailed and scraped
Round myriad warts that might be little hills.

From gloom's last dregs these long-strung creatures crept,
And vanished out of dawn down hidden holes.

(And smell came up from those foul openings
15 As out of mouths, or deep wounds deepening.)

On dithering feet upgathered, more and more,
Brown strings, towards strings of grey, with bristling spines,
All migrants from green fields, intent on mire.

Those that were grey, of more abundant spawns,
20 Ramped on the rest and ate them and were eaten.

I saw their bitten backs curve, loop, and straighten.
I watched those agonies curl, lift and flatten.

Whereat, in terror what that sight might mean,
I reeled and shivered earthward like a feather.

25 And Death fell with me, like a deepening moan.
    And He, picking a manner of worm, which half had hid
    Its bruises in the earth, but crawled no further,
    Showed me its feet, the feet of many men,
    And the fresh-severed head of it, my head.

Drafted at Scarborough in November 1917 and revised at Ripon in May 1918 (WO, 243–5), this is almost certainly the poem referred to in WO to SS, 27 November 1917: 'My "Vision" is the result of two hours' leisure yesterday, – and getting up early this morning! If you have objections to make, would you return it? If not, pass it on to R[obbie]. R[oss].' (CL, 512) That this 'Vision' was what came to be called 'The Show' (and not the fragment [CP&F, 481] 'A Vision in Whitechapel', later retitled 'Lines to a Beauty seen in Limehouse', as the editors of CL suggest) is made clear by WO to SS of 6 December 1917: 'What do you think of my Vowel-rime stunt in this ['Wild with all Regrets', to become 'A Terre' (p. 65)], and "Vision"?' (CL, 514)

WO's vision derives from his experience of battlefields between January and May 1917 (see notes to ll. 5 and 26–7 below) and from his reading in November–December 1917 of Henri Barbusse, *Under Fire* (1917). Chapter i of this is entitled 'The Vision':
'The man at the end of the rank cries, "I can see crawling things down there" – "Yes, as though they were alive" – "Some sort of plant perhaps" – "Some kind of men" –
'And there amid the baleful glimmers of the storm, below the dark disorder of the clouds that extend and unfurl over the earth like evil spirits, they seem to see a great livid plain unrolled, which to their seeing is made of mud and water, while figures appear and fast fix themselves to the surface of it, all blinded and borne down with filth, like the dreadful castaways of shipwreck.' (4)
'The Show' may also echo two passages from chapter xx: 'Dwarfed to the size of insects and worms, they make a queer dark stirring among these shadow-hidden and Death-pacified lands . . . (255); and 'In the middle of the plateau and in the depth of the rainy and bitter air, on the ghastly morrow of this debauch of slaughter, there is a head planted in the ground, a wet and bloodless head, with a heavy beard. It is one of ours, and the helmet is beside it.' (265)

TITLE 'Show' was soldiers' slang for 'battle'. Cp. 'The Chances' (p. 58) l. 1: 'the night before that show'.

EPIGRAPH WO misquotes Forgael's speech in Yeats's play *The Shadowy Waters (Poems 1899–1905* [1906], 22), which reads 'burnished mirror' (WO, 245). For WO's ironic use of Yeatsian epigraphs, see Jon Stallworthy, 'W. B. Yeats and Wilfred Owen', *Critical Quarterly*, xi, no. 3 [Autumn 1969], 199–214.)

4–5 Cp. WO to SO, 19 January 1917: '[No Man's Land] is pock-marked like a body of foulest disease and its odour is the

breath of cancer . . . No Man's Land under snow is like
the face of the moon chaotic, crater-ridden, uninhabitable, awful, the
abode of madness.' (CL, 429)

16–17 The caterpillars 'with bristling spines', are files of soldiers:
the Germans in grey uniforms, the British in khaki.

26–7 Cp. WO to CO, 14 May 1917: 'Then we were caught in a
Tornado of Shells. The various "waves" were all broken up
and we carried on like a crowd moving off a cricket-field.
When I looked back and saw the ground all crawling and
wormy with wounded bodies, I felt no horror at all but only
an immense exultation at having got through the Barrage.'
(CL, 458)

29 See the quotation from Barbusse, 265, above. As the
commander of a platoon advancing in single file, WO would
have been literally and figuratively its 'head'.

CP&F, 316

FUTILITY

Move him into the sun –
Gently its touch awoke him once,
At home, whispering of fields half-sown.
Always it woke him, even in France,
5 Until this morning and this snow.
If anything might rouse him now
The kind old sun will know.

Think how it wakes the seeds –
Woke once the clays of a cold star.
10 Are limbs, so dear achieved, are sides
Full-nerved, still warm, too hard to stir?
Was it for this the clay grew tall?
– O what made fatuous sunbeams toil
To break earth's sleep at all?

Written at Ripon in May 1918.

TITLE Cp. Tennyson, *In Memoriam*, lvi, l. 25: 'O life as futile, then, as frail!'
For a discussion of the influence of Tennyson's elegy on WO's, see DH,
Wilfred Owen (Writers and Their Work, 1975), 32–3.

3 half-sown: Previous editors read 'unsown'.

7 old sun: Cp. Donne, 'The Sun Rising', l. 1: 'Busy old fool, unruly sun'.

8–9 Cp. John Davidson, 'Thirty Bob a Week', ll. 71-2: 'A little sleeping seed,
I woke – I did, indeed – /A million years before the blooming sun.' Also
Sir Walter Scott, Hymn 487, *The English Hymnal*, ll. 9–12:
    O, on that day, that wrathful day,
    When man to judgement wakes from clay,
    Be thou the trembling sinner's stay,
    Though heaven and earth shall pass away!

CP&F, 319

THE END

After the blast of lightning from the east,
   The flourish of loud clouds, the Chariot Throne;
After the drums of time have rolled and ceased,
   And by the bronze west long retreat is blown,
5 Shall Life renew these bodies? Of a truth,
   All death will he annul, all tears assuage?
Or fill these void veins full again with youth,
   And wash, with an immortal water, age?

When I do ask white Age, he saith not so:
10   'My head hangs weighed with snow.'
And when I hearken to the Earth, she saith:
   'My fiery heart shrinks, aching. It is death.
Mine ancient scars shall not be glorified,
Nor my titanic tears, the seas, be dried.'

Begun probably in late 1916; continued either at Craiglockhart in
October–November 1917, or at Scarborough between November 1917 and
January 1918; this poem is almost certainly that referred to in WO's letter of 12
February 1917 to SO: 'Leslie tells me that Miss Joergens considers my Sonnet
on "The End" the finest of the lot. Naturally, because it is, intentionally, in her
style!' (CL, 434). 'To Eros' (JS, 92), was also, at one time, entitled 'The End',
as was the unfinished fragment on CP&F, 491. ELG's 'The End' was
published in *YM/The British Empire YMCA Weekly*, ii, no. 102 (22 December
1916), 1229. DH discusses WO's poem's debt to Shelley, *Prometheus Unbound*
(Wilfred Owen [Writers and Their Work, 1975], 19–20), and Hilda D. Spear its
refutation of the biblical Book of Revelation ('"I Too Saw God": The Religious
Allusions in Wilfred Owen's Poetry', *English*, xxiv, no. 119 [Summer 1975],
35–6).

    5–6 Cp. Revelation 21:4, 'And God shall wipe away all tears from their eyes;
        and there shall be no more death, neither sorrow, nor crying.' For the
        misquotation from WO's lines on his tombstone, see WO, 288.

    14 titanic tears: Cp. 'Strange Meeting' (p. 35), l. 3: 'titanic wars'.

CP&F, 322

S.I.W.

> I will to the King,
> And offer him consolation in his trouble,
> For that man there has set his teeth to die,
> And being one that hates obedience,
> Discipline, and orderliness of life,
> I cannot mourn him.
>
> W. B. YEATS

I   The Prologue

Patting goodbye, doubtless they told the lad
He'd always show the Hun a brave man's face;
Father would sooner him dead than in disgrace, –
Was proud to see him going, aye, and glad.
5 Perhaps his mother whimpered how she'd fret
Until he got a nice safe wound to nurse.
Sisters would wish girls too could shoot, charge, curse . . .
Brothers – would send his favourite cigarette.
Each week, month after month, they wrote the same,
10 Thinking him sheltered in some Y.M. Hut,
Because he said so, writing on his butt
Where once an hour a bullet missed its aim.
And misses teased the hunger of his brain.
His eyes grew old with wincing, and his hand
15 Reckless with ague. Courage leaked, as sand
From the best sandbags after years of rain.
But never leave, wound, fever, trench-foot, shock,
Untrapped the wretch. And death seemed still withheld
For torture of lying machinally shelled,
20 At the pleasure of this world's Powers who'd run amok.

He'd seen men shoot their hands, on night patrol.
Their people never knew. Yet they were vile.
'Death sooner than dishonour, that's the style!'
So Father said.

II   The Action

              One dawn, our wire patrol
25 Carried him. This time, Death had not missed.

We could do nothing but wipe his bleeding cough.
Could it be accident? – Rifles go off . . .
Not sniped? No. (Later they found the English ball.)

III The Poem

It was the reasoned crisis of his soul
30 Against more days of inescapable thrall,
Against infrangibly wired and blind trench wall
Curtained with fire, roofed in with creeping fire,
Slow grazing fire, that would not burn him whole
But kept him for death's promises and scoff,
35 And life's half-promising, and both their riling.

IV The Epilogue

With him they buried the muzzle his teeth had kissed,
And truthfully wrote the mother, 'Tim died smiling.'

Drafted at Craiglockhart in September 1917 and revised at Ripon in May 1918, this poem shows the influence of such poems by SS as 'The Hero' and 'Stand-to: Good Friday Morning'.

TITLE Military abbreviation for 'Self-Inflicted Wound'.

EPIGRAPH From Yeats's play, *The King's Threshold, Poems 1899–1905* (1906), 238. (For WO's ironic use of Yeatsian epigraphs, see Jon Stallworthy, 'W. B. Yeats and Wilfred Owen', *Critical Quarterly*, xi, no. 3 [Autumn 1969], 199–214.)

10 Y.M. Hut: Young Men's Christian Association hostel.

31 blind trench: one with no outlet.

32 creeping fire: A 'creeping barrage' advanced a predetermined distance – usually in front of advancing infantry – at a predetermined time.

THE CALLS

A dismal fog-hoarse siren howls at dawn.
I watch the man it calls for, pushed and drawn
Backwards and forwards, helpless as a pawn.
    But I'm lazy, and his work's crazy.

5 Quick treble bells begin at nine o'clock,
Scuttling the schoolboy pulling up his sock,
Scaring the late girl in the inky frock.
    I must be crazy; I learn from the daisy.

Stern bells annoy the rooks and doves at ten.
10 I watch the verger close the doors, and when
I hear the organ moan the first amen,
    Sing my religion's – same as pigeons'.

A blatant bugle tears my afternoons.
Out clump the clumsy Tommies by platoons,
15 Trying to keep in step with rag-time tunes,
    But I sit still; I've done my drill.

Gongs hum and buzz like saucepan-lids at dusk.
I see a food-hog whet his gold-filled tusk
To eat less bread, and more luxurious rusk.

20 Then sometimes late at night my window bumps
From gunnery-practice, till my small heart thumps
And listens for the shell-shrieks and the crumps,
    But that's not all.

For leaning out last midnight on my sill,
25 I heard the sighs of men, that have no skill
To speak of their distress, no, nor the will!
    A voice I know. And this time I must go.

Revised – it may have been written earlier – at Scarborough in May 1918 (wo,
266), and here treated as a poem rather than a fragment – although the
manuscript makes clear that its revisions are incomplete – since it has gained

currency as such from its appearance in CDL and DH. On 10 August 1918, WO wrote to SO: 'Tomorrow I am for a medical inspection with 21 others, to be declared fit for draft. This means we may be sent on draft leave tomorrow, & I may reach you even before this letter! I know not. I am glad. That is I am much gladder to be going out again than afraid. I shall be better able to cry my outcry, playing my part.' (CL, 568)

18–19 food-hog: Perhaps a reference to 'the stinking Leeds & Bradford War-profiteers' mentioned in the letter to SO quoted above. DH notes that '"Eat less bread" was a widespread slogan in the Food Economy Campaign in 1917. One poster reads, "Save the Wheat / and / Help the Fleet. / Eat / Less / Bread." The Food Controller sent a circular to households in May 1917 and said, "We must all eat less food, especially we must all eat less bread".' ('Some Contemporary Allusions in Poems by Rosenberg, Owen and Sassoon', N&Q, n.s., xxvi, no. 4 (August 1979), 333–4)

19 The MS shows two cancelled attempts at a line following this, and one must suppose that WO intended to try again.

23 Cancelled attempts at this line suggest that WO intended 'But that's not all' to be only its second half.

CP&F, 332

TRAINING

Not this week nor this month dare I lie down
In languor under lime trees or smooth smile.
Love must not kiss my face pale that is brown.

My lips, panting, shall drink space, mile by mile;
5   Strong meats be all my hunger; my renown
Be the clean beauty of speed and pride of style.

Cold winds encountered on the racing Down
Shall thrill my heated bareness; but awhile
None else may meet me till I wear my crown.

Written, probably at Scarborough, in June 1918 (the date on the MS). WO
arrived in Scarborough, from Ripon, on 5 June and on 1 July 1918 wrote to SO:
'Went a Cross Country Run last Wednesday, from which my calves are still
suffering. Have seldom enjoyed any exercise so much.' (CL, 561)

    4 panting: EB and CDL read 'parting', which also fits the context, but is
       not, I think, what WO wrote.

    9 Cp. WO to OS, July 1918: 'For 14 hours yesterday I was at work –
       teaching Christ to lift his cross by numbers, and how to adjust his
       crown' (CL, 562).

CP&F, 334

THE NEXT WAR

War's a joke for me and you,
While we know such dreams are true.
SIEGFRIED SASSOON

Out there, we walked quite friendly up to Death, –
   Sat down and ate beside him, cool and bland, –
   Pardoned his spilling mess-tins in our hand.
We've sniffed the green thick odour of his breath, –
5 Our eyes wept, but our courage didn't writhe.
   He's spat at us with bullets, and he's coughed
   Shrapnel. We chorused if he sang aloft,
We whistled while he shaved us with his scythe.

Oh, Death was never enemy of ours!
10   We laughed at him, we leagued with him, old chum.
No soldier's paid to kick against His powers.
   We laughed, – knowing that better men would come,
And greater wars: when every fighter brags
He fights on Death, for lives; not men, for flags.

Written at Craiglockhart in late September 1917 and sent, with 'Anthem for Doomed Youth' (p. 12), to SO on the 25th (CL, 496). On 2 October 1917, WO told her: 'I included my "Next War" in order to strike a note. I want Colin to read, mark, learn etc. it.' (CL, 497) The poem was revised at Scarborough in July 1918.

EPIGRAPH SS, 'A Letter Home' (to Robert Graves, written at Flixécourt in May 1916), ll. 73–4.

    14 on: against.

CP&F, 334

GREATER LOVE

Red lips are not so red
   As the stained stones kissed by the English dead.
Kindness of wooed and wooer
Seems shame to their love pure.
5 O Love, your eyes lose lure
   When I behold eyes blinded in my stead!

Your slender attitude
   Trembles not exquisite like limbs knife-skewed,
Rolling and rolling there
10 Where God seems not to care;
Till the fierce love they bear
   Cramps them in death's extreme decrepitude.

Your voice sings not so soft, –
   Though even as wind murmuring through raftered loft, –
15 Your dear voice is not dear,
Gentle, and evening clear,
As theirs whom none now hear,
   Now earth has stopped their piteous mouths that coughed.

Heart, you were never hot
20 Nor large, nor full like hearts made great with shot;
And though your hand be pale,
Paler are all which trail
Your cross through flame and hail:
   Weep, you may weep, for you may touch them not.

Drafted either at Craiglockhart in October–November 1917 (WO, 230–1), or at
Scarborough between November 1917 and January 1918, and revised at
Scarborough that July, the poem is a response to Swinburne's poem 'Before the
Mirror / (Verses Written under a Picture) / Inscribed to J. A. Whistler', ll. 1–7:
   White Rose in red rose-garden
     Is not so white;
   Snowdrops that plead for pardon
     And pine for fright
   Because the hard East blows
   Over their maiden rows
     Grow not as this face grows from pale to bright.

WO may also have been aware of Salomé's words to Jokanaan in Wilde's *Salomé*: 'The roses in the garden of the Queen of Arabia are not so white as thy body.' WO had written to SO on 16 [?] May 1917: 'Christ is literally in no man's land. There men often hear His voice: Greater love hath no man than this, that a man lay down his life – for a friend.' (CL, 461)

TITLE   Cp. John 15:13: 'Greater love hath no man than this, that a man lay down his life for his friends.' See also 'At a Calvary near the Ancre' (p. 23), ll. 11–12: 'But they who love the greater love / Lay down their life; they do not hate.'

20   Cp. Elizabeth Barrett Browning, *Aurora Leigh*, Second Book, ll. 718–20:
> As my blood recoiled
> From that imputed ignominy, I made
> My heart great with it.

See also WO to SO, 2 April 1916: 'And the drums pulse fearfully-voluptuously, as great hearts in death' (CL, 388).

21   pale: Cp. Swinburne, 'Before the Mirror', quoted above.

22   trail: Used in the military sense of 'trail arms', carry a rifle with butt end near the ground and muzzle pointing forwards.

24   Cp. John 21:15–17: 'Jesus saith unto [Mary Magdalene], Woman, why weepest thou? . . . Jesus saith unto her, Touch me not; for I am not yet ascended to my Father.'

CP&F, 337

THE LAST LAUGH

'Oh! Jesus Christ! I'm hit,' he said; and died.
Whether he vainly cursed or prayed indeed,
      The Bullets chirped – In vain, vain, vain!
      Machine-guns chuckled – Tut-tut! Tut-tut!
5   And the Big Gun guffawed.

Another sighed – 'O Mother, – Mother, – Dad!'
Then smiled at nothing, childlike, being dead.
      And the lofty Shrapnel-cloud
      Leisurely gestured, – Fool!
10   And the splinters spat, and tittered.

'My Love!' one moaned. Love-languid seemed his mood,
Till slowly lowered, his whole face kissed the mud.
      And the Bayonets' long teeth grinned;
      Rabbles of Shells hooted and groaned;
15   And the Gas hissed.

Drafted at Scarborough in February 1918, an early version of this poem was
included in WO's letter of 18 February to SO, and was there prefaced: 'There
is a point where prayer is indistinguishable from blasphemy. There is also a
point where blasphemy is indistinguishable from prayer. As in this first verse . . .'
(CL, 534) The first of the three later drafts, in which full rhymes have given
place to pararhymes, is dated '5.3.18', and WO's subsequent revisions must
date from spring–summer 1918 when he gave a final fair copy to OS.

CP&F, 341

MENTAL CASES

Who are these? Why sit they here in twilight?
Wherefore rock they, purgatorial shadows,
Drooping tongues from jaws that slob their relish,
Baring teeth that leer like skulls' teeth wicked?
5   Stroke on stroke of pain, – but what slow panic,
Gouged these chasms round their fretted sockets?
Ever from their hair and through their hands' palms
Misery swelters. Surely we have perished
Sleeping, and walk hell; but who these hellish?

10 – These are men whose minds the Dead have ravished.
Memory fingers in their hair of murders,
Multitudinous murders they once witnessed.
Wading sloughs of flesh these helpless wander,
Treading blood from lungs that had loved laughter.
15   Always they must see these things and hear them,
Batter of guns and shatter of flying muscles,
Carnage incomparable, and human squander
Rucked too thick for these men's extrication.

Therefore still their eyeballs shrink tormented
20 Back into their brains, because on their sense
Sunlight seems a blood-smear; night comes blood-black;
Dawn breaks open like a wound that bleeds afresh.
– Thus their heads wear this hilarious, hideous,
Awful falseness of set-smiling corpses.
25 – Thus their hands are plucking at each other;
Picking at the rope-knouts of their scourging;
Snatching after us who smote them, brother,
Pawing us who dealt them war and madness.

Drafted at Ripon in May 1918 and revised at Scarborough in July, this poem
draws on the earlier fragment, 'Purgatorial Passions' (CP&F, 455). WO wrote
to SO on 25 May: 'I've been "busy" this evening with my terrific poem (at
present) called "The Deranged". This poem the Editor of the *Burlington
Magazine* – (a 2/6 Arts Journal which takes no poetry) – old More Adey, I say,
solemnly prohibited me from sending to the English Review, on the grounds that
"the *English Review* should not be encouraged".!!!!' (CL, 553) On 15 June 1918

he told SO: 'lo! an urgent request from the Sitwells in London for more of my poems for their 1918 Anthology which is coming out immediately. This is on the strength of "The Deranged", which S. Moncrieff showed them the other day.' (CL, 559) In the event, the Sitwells printed no poems by WO in their anthology *Wheels* (1918).

The poem reflects WO's reading of Dante, and Mr Mark Sinfield points out (in a letter to the editor) that the opening of each stanza echoes the diction and, with bitter irony, parallels the structure of the King James version of Revelation 7:13–17: 'What are these which are arrayed in white robes? and whence came they? . . . These are they which came out of great tribulation, and have washed their robes, and made them white in the blood of the Lamb. Therefore are they before the throne of God, and serve him day and night in his temple: and he that sitteth on the throne shall dwell among them. They shall hunger no more, neither thirst any more; neither shall the sun light on them, nor any heat. For the Lamb which is in the midst of the throne shall feed them, and shall lead them unto living fountains of waters: and God shall wipe away all tears from their eyes.'

12 Multitudinous murders: Cp. *Macbeth*, 11. ii. 58–60:
>   No; this my hand will rather
> The multitudinous seas incarnadine,
> Making the green one red.

19 The MS variants of this line confirm the impression that this poem owes something to the influence of Isaac Watts, 'The Day of Judgement', ll. 17–24:

> Hark, the shrill outcries of the guilty wretches!
> Lively bright horror, and amazing anguish,
> Stare thro' their eye-lids, while the living worm lies
>   Gnawing within them.

> Thoughts, like old vultures, prey upon their heart-strings,
> And the smart twinges, when the eye beholds the
> Lofty Judge frowning, and a flood of vengeance
>   Rolling afore him.

26 Cp. 'The Rime of the Youthful Mariner' (JS, 108), ll. 1–3.

CP&F, 342

THE CHANCES

I 'mind as how the night before that show
Us five got talkin'; we was in the know.
'Ah well,' says Jimmy, and he's seen some scrappin',
'There ain't no more than five things as can happen, –
5 You get knocked out; else wounded, bad or cushy;
Scuppered; or nowt except you're feelin' mushy.'

One of us got the knock-out, blown to chops;
One lad was hurt, like, losin' both his props;
And one – to use the word of hypocrites –
10 Had the misfortune to be took by Fritz.
Now me, I wasn't scratched, praise God Almighty,
Though next time please I'll thank Him for a blighty.
But poor old Jim, he's livin' and he's not;
He reckoned he'd five chances, and he had:
15 He's wounded, killed, and pris'ner, all the lot,
The flamin' lot all rolled in one. Jim's mad.

Drafted at Craiglockhart in August–September 1917, this poem shows the
strong influence of SS. It was revised at Scarborough in July 1918.
    1 show: Soldiers' slang for 'battle'.
    2 Previous editors follow this line with a couplet omitted from the final
       version.
    5 cushy: Soldiers' slang for 'slightly'.
    6 scuppered: Soldiers' (from nautical) slang for 'killed'.
       nowt: Dialect for 'nothing'.
    8 props: Soldiers' slang for 'legs'.
  10 Fritz: Soldiers' slang for 'the Germans'.
  12 blighty: A wound serious enough to cause a soldier to be sent back to
       England.

CP&F, 345

[58]

THE SEND-OFF

Down the close darkening lanes they sang their way
To the siding-shed,
And lined the train with faces grimly gay.

Their breasts were stuck all white with wreath and spray
5   As men's are, dead.

Dull porters watched them, and a casual tramp
Stood staring hard,
Sorry to miss them from the upland camp.

Then, unmoved, signals nodded, and a lamp
10   Winked to the guard.

So secretly, like wrongs hushed-up, they went.
They were not ours:
We never heard to which front these were sent;

Nor there if they yet mock what women meant
15   Who gave them flowers.

Shall they return to beating of great bells
In wild train-loads?
A few, a few, too few for drums and yells,

May creep back, silent, to village wells,
20   Up half-known roads.

Drafted at Ripon in April–May 1918 (WO, 261–2), and revised at Scarborough
in July, this may be one of the 'two poems' mentioned in WO's letter to ELG
of 21 April 1918 (CL, 547). On 4 May he was able to tell SO: 'I have long
"waited" for a final stanza to "the Draft" (which begins:

I

"Down the deep, darkening lanes they sang their way
To the waiting train,
And filled its doors with faces grimly gay,
And heads & shoulders white with wreath & spray,
As men's are, slain.")

*   *   *

IV

Will they return, to beatings of great bells,
In wild train-loads?
– A few, a few, too few for drums and yells,
May walk back, silent, to their village wells,
Up half-known roads.'

(CL., 550)

6–8 Bäckman observes (43): 'These lines contain a couple of ironic echoes
of stanzas 25 and 27 of Gray's "Elegy", where a "hoary-headed swain"
is heard to say that he had often seen the departed country poet
"brushing with hasty steps the dews away, / To meet the sun upon *the
upland lawn*", but then suddenly "one morn", he "*miss'd* him on the
custom'd hill". The hoary-headed swain in Gray's lines about the death
of an unknown poet becomes "a casual tramp" in Owen's poem
commemorating the departure of some soldiers for the front, and Gray's
poetic "upland lawn" becomes the more prosaic "upland camp".'
19 Previous editors read 'still village wells'.

CP&F, 346

THE PARABLE OF THE OLD MAN AND THE YOUNG

So Abram rose, and clave the wood, and went,
And took the fire with him, and a knife.
And as they sojourned both of them together,
Isaac the first-born spake and said, My Father,
5 Behold the preparations, fire and iron,
But where the lamb, for this burnt-offering?
Then Abram bound the youth with belts and straps,
And builded parapets and trenches there,
And stretchèd forth the knife to slay his son.
10 When lo! an Angel called him out of heaven,
Saying, Lay not thy hand upon the lad,
Neither do anything to him, thy son.
Behold! Caught in a thicket by its horns,
A Ram. Offer the Ram of Pride instead.

15 But the old man would not so, but slew his son,
And half the seed of Europe, one by one.

Written, probably at Scarborough, in July 1918, the poem's ll. 1–14 follow the
wording of Genesis 22:1–19 very closely.

    7 belts and straps: As of a soldier's equipment.
12–14 Previous editors print an earlier form of these lines.
    16 seed: Cp. '1914' (p. 16), l. 14: 'blood for seed'.

CP&F, 350

DISABLED

He sat in a wheeled chair, waiting for dark,
And shivered in his ghastly suit of grey,
Legless, sewn short at elbow. Through the park
Voices of boys rang saddening like a hymn,
5 Voices of play and pleasure after day,
Till gathering sleep had mothered them from him.

*   *   *

About this time Town used to swing so gay
When glow-lamps budded in the light blue trees,
And girls glanced lovelier as the air grew dim, –
10 In the old times, before he threw away his knees.
Now he will never feel again how slim
Girls' waists are, or how warm their subtle hands.
All of them touch him like some queer disease.

*   *   *

There was an artist silly for his face,
15 For it was younger than his youth, last year.
Now, he is old; his back will never brace;
He's lost his colour very far from here,
Poured it down shell-holes till the veins ran dry,
And half his lifetime lapsed in the hot race
20 And leap of purple spurted from his thigh.

*   *   *

One time he liked a blood-smear down his leg,
After the matches, carried shoulder-high.
It was after football, when he'd drunk a peg,
He thought he'd better join. – He wonders why.
25 Someone had said he'd look a god in kilts,
That's why; and maybe, too, to please his Meg,
Aye, that was it, to please the giddy jilts
He asked to join. He didn't have to beg;
Smiling they wrote his lie: aged nineteen years.

30 Germans he scarcely thought of; all their guilt,
And Austria's, did not move him. And no fears
Of Fear came yet. He thought of jewelled hilts
For daggers in plaid socks; of smart salutes;
And care of arms; and leave; and pay arrears;
35 Esprit de corps; and hints for young recruits.
And soon, he was drafted out with drums and cheers.

*   *   *

Some cheered him home, but not as crowds cheer Goal.
Only a solemn man who brought him fruits
Thanked him; and then enquired about his soul.

*   *   *

40 Now, he will spend a few sick years in institutes,
And do what things the rules consider wise,
And take whatever pity they may dole.
Tonight he noticed how the women's eyes
Passed from him to the strong men that were whole.
45 How cold and late it is! Why don't they come
And put him into bed? Why don't they come?

Drafted at Craiglockhart in October 1917 (WO, 224–6), and revised at
Scarborough in July 1918. On 14 October 1917 WO wrote to SO: 'On Sat. I
met Robert Graves ... No doubt he thought me a slacker sort of sub. S.S.
when they were together showed him my longish war-piece "Disabled" (you
haven't seen it) & it seems Graves was mightily impressed, and considers me a
kind of Find!! No thanks, Captain Graves! I'll find myself in due time.' (CL, 499)
On 18 October he told SO that Graves had 'carried away a Poem, or was
carried away with it, without my knowledge. It was only in a Draft State, & I was
perfectly aware of all the solecisms.' (CL, 501) A day or two earlier, Graves had
written to WO about that 'damn fine poem of yours, that "Disabled" ' (CL, 595).

22 Cp. A. E. Housman, 'To an Athlete Dying Young', ll. 1–4:
The time you won your town the race
We chaired you through the market-place;
Man and boy stood cheering by,
And home we brought you shoulder-high.

23 peg: slang expression for a drink, usually brandy and soda.

27 jilts: capricious women.

29 they wrote his lie: the recruiting officers entered on his enlistment form his lie that he was nineteen years old and therefore above the minimum age for military service.

45–6 DH calls attention to 'a mocking echo of the slogan on a recruiting poster, probably put out in 1914, which shows soldiers in action and in need of reinforcements. The slogan reads, "Will they never come?" . . . The parallel in this poem between playing football and serving in the Army reflects the recruiting drives that had been made at football matches earlier in the war. The Imperial War Museum preserves the following rather amateur poster: "Men of Millwall / Hundreds of Football enthusiasts / are joining the Army daily. / Don't be left behind. / Let the Enemy hear the 'LION'S ROAR'. Join and be in at THE FINAL / and give them a / KICK OFF THE EARTH".' ('Some Contemporary Allusions in Poems by Rosenberg, Owen and Sassoon', N&Q, n.s., xxvi, no. 4 [August 1979], 333)

CP&F, 351

A TERRE

(being the philosophy of many soldiers)

Sit on the bed. I'm blind, and three parts shell.
Be careful; can't shake hands now; never shall.
Both arms have mutinied against me, – brutes.
My fingers fidget like ten idle brats.

5   I tried to peg out soldierly, – no use!
One dies of war like any old disease.
This bandage feels like pennies on my eyes.
I have my medals? – Discs to make eyes close.
My glorious ribbons? – Ripped from my own back
10 In scarlet shreds. (That's for your poetry book.)

A short life and a merry one, my buck!
We used to say we'd hate to live dead-old, –
Yet now . . . I'd willingly be puffy, bald,
And patriotic. Buffers catch from boys
15 At least the jokes hurled at them. I suppose
Little I'd ever teach a son, but hitting,
Shooting, war, hunting, all the arts of hurting.
Well, that's what I learnt, – that, and making money.

Your fifty years ahead seem none too many?
20 Tell me how long I've got? God! For one year
To help myself to nothing more than air!
One Spring! Is one too good to spare, too long?
Spring wind would work its own way to my lung,
And grow me legs as quick as lilac-shoots.

25 My servant's lamed, but listen how he shouts!
When I'm lugged out, he'll still be good for that.
Here in this mummy-case, you know, I've thought
How well I might have swept his floors for ever.
I'd ask no nights off when the bustle's over,
30 Enjoying so the dirt. Who's prejudiced
Against a grimed hand when his own's quite dust,
Less live than specks that in the sun-shafts turn,
Less warm than dust that mixes with arms' tan?

I'd love to be a sweep, now, black as Town,
35   Yes, or a muckman. Must I be his load?

O Life, Life, let me breathe, – a dug-out rat!
Not worse than ours the lives rats lead –
Nosing along at night down some safe rut,
They find a shell-proof home before they rot.
40   Dead men may envy living mites in cheese,
Or good germs even. Microbes have their joys,
And subdivide, and never come to death.
Certainly flowers have the easiest time on earth.
'I shall be one with nature, herb, and stone,'
45   Shelley would tell me. Shelley would be stunned:
The dullest Tommy hugs that fancy now.
'Pushing up daisies' is their creed, you know.

To grain, then, go my fat, to buds my sap,
For all the usefulness there is in soap.
50   D'you think the Boche will ever stew man-soup?
Some day, no doubt, if . . .
                                    Friend, be very sure
I shall be better off with plants that share
More peaceably the meadow and the shower.
Soft rains will touch me, – as they could touch once,
55   And nothing but the sun shall make me ware.
Your guns may crash around me. I'll not hear;
Or, if I wince, I shall not know I wince.

Don't take my soul's poor comfort for your jest.
Soldiers may grow a soul when turned to fronds,
60   But here the thing's best left at home with friends.

My soul's a little grief, grappling your chest,
To climb your throat on sobs; easily chased
On other sighs and wiped by fresher winds.

Carry my crying spirit till it's weaned
65   To do without what blood remained these wounds.

Begun at Scarborough in December 1917 (WO, 248), and revised there in July 1918. On 3 December 1917 WO told SO: 'I finished an important poem this afternoon' (CL, 513), and three days later he wrote to SS: 'This "Wild with all Regrets" was begun & ended two days ago, at one gasp. If simplicity, if imaginativeness, if sympathy, if resonance of vowels, make poetry I have not succeeded. But if you say "Here is poetry," it will be so for me. What do you think of my Vowel-rime stunt in this, and "Vision"? Do you consider the hop from Flea to Soul too abrupt?' (CL, 514) At Ripon, in April 1918, 'Wild with all Regrets' was expanded into 'A Terre'.

7 pennies: It was once customary to place coins on the eyelids of a corpse to keep them closed.

13–14 Cp. SS, 'Base Details', ll. 1–4:
    If I were fierce, and bald, and short of breath,
        I'd live with scarlet Majors at the Base,
    And speed glum heroes up the line to death.
        You'd see me with my puffy petulant face . . .

19 Cp. A. E. Housman, 'Loveliest of trees, the cherry now', ll. 9–12:
    And since to look at things in bloom
    Fifty springs are little room,
    About the woodlands I will go
    To see the cherry hung with snow.

30 dirt: Cp. 'Inspection' (p.10), l. 8: '"Well, blood is dirt," I said.'

34 sweep: chimney-sweep.

36 Cp. King Lear, v. iii. 307–8: 'Why should a dog, a horse, a rat, have life, / And thou no breath at all?'

37 lives: Previous editors read 'existences', but see CP&F, 354.

44 The quotation is from Shelley, 'Adonais', xlii:
    He is made one with Nature: there is heard
    His voice in all her music, from the moan
    Of thunder, to the song of night's sweet bird;
    He is a presence to be felt and known
    In darkness and in light, from herb and stone.
    Spreading itself where'er that Power may move
    Which has withdrawn his being to its own . . .

47 'Pushing up daisies': A common slang expression, meaning dead.

48–50 Cp. SS, 'The Tombstone-Maker', ll. 11–12: 'I told him with a sympathetic grin, / That Germans boil dead soldiers down for fat.'

54–5 Cp. 'Futility' (p. 45), ll. 1–2: 'Move him into the sun – / Gently its touch awoke him once. . .'

59 Cp. 'Miners' (p.24), l. 7: 'Frond-forests'.

CP&F, 354

THE KIND GHOSTS

She sleeps on soft, last breaths; but no ghost looms
Out of the stillness of her palace wall,
Her wall of boys on boys and dooms on dooms.

She dreams of golden gardens and sweet glooms,
5 Not marvelling why her roses never fall
Nor what red mouths were torn to make their blooms.

The shades keep down which well might roam her hall.
Quiet their blood lies in her crimson rooms
And she is not afraid of their footfall.

10 They move not from her tapestries, their pall,
Nor pace her terraces, their hecatombs,
Lest aught she be disturbed, or grieved at all.

Revised – it may have been written earlier – at Scarborough on 30 July 1918,
according to the dated MS, this may be the poem referred to in WO's letter to
SO of 8 August 1918 (CL, 567).

    1 She: Probably Britannia. DH notes that 'The word "Brittannia" (Owen's
spelling was erratic) appears unexplained in a rough list of titles which he
jotted down that summer; it seems likely to have been a draft title for this
poem. Compare Swinburne's "Perinde ac Cadaver". While he was in
France he acquired a copy of Swinburne's *Poems and Ballads*; it was
probably the last book he read' (*Wilfred Owen* [Writers and Their Work,
1975], 35).

    11 hecatombs: 'great public sacrifices' (*OED*). WO may have meant 'places
of great public sacrifice'. Alternatively, he may have used the word,
incorrectly, to mean 'tombs' or confused it with 'catacombs'.

SOLDIER'S DREAM

I dreamed kind Jesus fouled the big-gun gears;
And caused a permanent stoppage in all bolts;
And buckled with a smile Mausers and Colts;
And rusted every bayonet with His tears.

5 And there were no more bombs, of ours or Theirs,
Not even an old flint-lock, nor even a pikel.
But God was vexed, and gave all power to Michael;
And when I woke he'd seen to our repairs.

Begun at Craiglockhart in October 1917 and revised at Scarborough, probably
that November and in July–August 1918. On 27 November 1917, WO wrote to
SS: 'I trust you'll like the "Soldier's Dream" well enough to pass it on to the
Nation or Cambridge? This was the last piece from Craiglockhart.' (CL, 512)

   3 Mausers and Colts: German and American brands of revolver.

   6 flint-lock: Old-fashioned gun with a flint in the hammer for striking a
      spark to ignite a charge of gunpowder.
      pikel: 'hay-fork or pitchfork' (*OED*), but perhaps here meant to suggest
      'bayonet'.

   7 Michael: The Archangel commanding the heavenly armies.

CP&F, 358

ELEGY IN APRIL AND SEPTEMBER

(jabbered among the trees)

1

Hush, thrush! Hush, missel-thrush, I listen . . .
I heard the flush of footsteps through loose leaves,
And a low whistle by the water's brim.

Still! daffodil! Nay, hail me not so gaily,–
5 Your gay gold lily daunts me and deceives,
Who follow gleams more golden and more slim.

Look, brook! O run and look, O run!
The vain reeds shook? – Yet search till grey sea heaves,
And I will stray among these fields for him.

10 Gaze, daisy! Stare through haze and glare,
And mark the hazardous stars all dawns and eves,
For my eye withers, and his star wanes dim.

2

Close, rose, and droop, heliotrope,
And shudder, hope! The shattering winter blows.
15 Drop, heliotrope, and close, rose . . .

Mourn, corn, and sigh, rye.
Men garner you, but youth's head lies forlorn.
Sigh, rye, and mourn, corn . . .

Brood, wood, and muse, yews,
20 The ways gods use we have not understood.
Muse, yews, and brood, wood . . .

Begun at Ripon in April–May 1918, this attempt at a pastoral elegy was
continued in France the following September. On the back of one MS, WO has
written 'Mat[t]hew Arnold' and beneath that a list beginning 'Thyr[s]is /
Scholar Gipsy'; and it would seem that WO had Arnold's elegies in mind as
models for his own. CDL prints only an earlier version of ll. 1–12.

    TITLE The subject of this elegy – in one draft described as 'a Poet . . . reported
        killed' – has not been identified.

      1 missel-thrush: WO wrote (and CDL reproduces his error) 'missen-thrush'.

EXPOSURE

Our brains ache, in the merciless iced east winds that knive us . . .
Wearied we keep awake because the night is silent . . .
Low, drooping flares confuse our memory of the salient . . .
Worried by silence, sentries whisper, curious, nervous,
        But nothing happens.

Watching, we hear the mad gusts tugging on the wire,
Like twitching agonies of men among its brambles.
Northward, incessantly, the flickering gunnery rumbles,
Far off, like a dull rumour of some other war.
        What are we doing here?

The poignant misery of dawn begins to grow . . .
We only know war lasts, rain soaks, and clouds sag stormy.
Dawn massing in the east her melancholy army
Attacks once more in ranks on shivering ranks of grey,
        But nothing happens.

Sudden successive flights of bullets streak the silence.
Less deathly than the air that shudders black with snow,
With sidelong flowing flakes that flock, pause, and renew;
We watch them wandering up and down the wind's nonchalance,
        But nothing happens.

Pale flakes with fingering stealth come feeling for our faces –
We cringe in holes, back on forgotten dreams, and stare, snow-dazed,
Deep into grassier ditches. So we drowse, sun-dozed,
Littered with blossoms trickling where the blackbird fusses,
        – Is it that we are dying?

Slowly our ghosts drag home: glimpsing the sunk fires, glozed
With crusted dark-red jewels; crickets jingle there;
For hours the innocent mice rejoice: the house is theirs;
Shutters and doors, all closed: on us the doors are closed, –
        We turn back to our dying.

Since we believe not otherwise can kind fires burn;
Nor ever suns smile true on child, or field, or fruit.
For God's invincible spring our love is made afraid;
Therefore, not loath, we lie out here; therefore were born,
35   For love of God seems dying.

Tonight, this frost will fasten on this mud and us,
Shrivelling many hands, puckering foreheads crisp.
The burying-party, picks and shovels in shaking grasp,
Pause over half-known faces. All their eyes are ice,
40   But nothing happens.

Begun at Scarborough in December 1917, when one unfinished line was written at the top of the MS of the fragment 'Cramped in that funnelled hole . . .' (p. 89); revised there in early 1918; and finished in France in September 1918, when its final draft was written on the same paper as that used for the second draft of 'Elegy in April and September' (p. 70), which was composed in that month. WO appears to have dated the final draft of 'Exposure' 'Feb. 1916', but the '6' could be an imperfect '8' (WO, 246–8). EB suggested that WO may have intended to write 'Feb. 1917', since the poem stems from experiences described in a letter to SO dated 4 February 1917. (See DH, 'The Date of Wilfred Owen's "Exposure"', N&Q, n.s., xxiii, no. 7 [July 1976], 305–8.) On 22 April 1918, WO wrote to SO: 'to quote myself cynically "Nothing happens"' (CL, 548), which suggests that 'Exposure' was far enough advanced for her to be expected to recognize its refrain. It appears, under the title 'Nothing happens', in one of the lists of contents drawn up at Ripon between March and June 1918 (see CP&F, 539).

  1 An ironic echo of Keats, 'Ode to a Nightingale', ll. 1–2: 'My heart aches, and a drowsy numbness pains / My sense.'

  3 salient: The front line in places jutted into enemy territory, and at such 'salients' the fighting tended to be fiercest.

  9 Cp. Matthew 24:6: 'wars and rumours of wars'; also WO to ELG, 25 July 1915: 'You say you "hear of wars and rumours of wars". *Vous en êtes là seulement?* You hear Rumours? The rumours, over here, make the ears of the gunners bleed.' (CL, 349)

14 grey: The German troops wore grey uniforms and, like the dawn, came from the east.

22 Cp. 'Cramped in that funnelled hole . . .' (p. 89).

23 drowse: See note on l. 1 above.

26 Cp. the song: 'Keep the homes fire burning . . . Though your lads are far away they dream of home.'
glozed: A conflation of 'glowing' and 'glazed'.

29 DH, in "The Date of Wilfred Owen's "Exposure"', suggests a link with WO's postcard of 24 November 1917 to SO, in which he describes how he found himself at York in the small hours of the morning. The Station Hotel was full and 'the other hotels would not open to my knocking' (CL, 508).

33 God's invincible spring: Cp. the fragment 'The Wrestlers' (p. 90): 'And all the ardour of the invincible spring'.

36 SS, EB, and CDL print 'His frost', an attractive but inaccurate reading.

39 All their eyes are ice: Cp. Yeats, 'The Happy Townland', l. 11: 'Queens, their eyes blue like the ice'.

CP&F, 365

THE SENTRY

We'd found an old Boche dug-out, and he knew,
And gave us hell; for shell on frantic shell
Lit full on top, but never quite burst through.
Rain, guttering down in waterfalls of slime,
5 Kept slush waist-high and rising hour by hour,
And choked the steps too thick with clay to climb.
What murk of air remained stank old, and sour
With fumes from whizz-bangs, and the smell of men
Who'd lived there years, and left their curse in the den,
10 If not their corpses . . .
               There we herded from the blast
Of whizz-bangs; but one found our door at last, –
Buffeting eyes and breath, snuffing the candles,
And thud! flump! thud! down the steep steps came thumping
And sploshing in the flood, deluging muck,
15 The sentry's body; then his rifle, handles
Of old Boche bombs, and mud in ruck on ruck.
We dredged it up, for dead, until he whined,
'O sir – my eyes, – I'm blind, – I'm blind, – I'm blind.'
Coaxing, I held a flame against his lids
20 And said if he could see the least blurred light
He was not blind; in time they'd get all right.
'I can't,' he sobbed. Eyeballs, huge-bulged like squids',
Watch my dreams still, – yet I forgot him there
In posting Next for duty, and sending a scout
25 To beg a stretcher somewhere, and flound'ring about
To other posts under the shrieking air.

Those other wretches, how they bled and spewed,
And one who would have drowned himself for good, –
I try not to remember these things now.
30 Let Dread hark back for one word only: how,
Half-listening to that sentry's moans and jumps,
And the wild chattering of his shivered teeth,
Renewed most horribly whenever crumps

Pummelled the roof and slogged the air beneath, –
35 Through the dense din, I say, we heard him shout
'I see your lights!' – But ours had long gone out.

Begun at Craiglockhart between August and October 1917, continued at
Scarborough in May 1918, and completed in France that September (WO, 274),
this must be one of the 'few poems' that accompanied WO's letter of 22
September 1918 to SS (CL, 578). A year and a half before, on 16 January 1917,
he had written to SO: 'In the Platoon on my left the sentries over the dug-out
were blown to nothing. One of these poor fellows was my first servant whom I
rejected. If I had kept him he would have lived, for servants don't do Sentry
Duty. I kept my own sentries half way down the stairs during the more terrific
bombardment. In spite of this one lad was blown down and, I am afraid,
blinded' (CL, 428). Previous editors follow an earlier MS.

   8 whizz-bangs: Small shells of such high velocity that the sound made in
      passing through the air is almost simultaneous with the explosion.
  22 Eyeballs: Cp. the other tormented eyes that stare from 'Dulce et
      Decorum Est' (p. 29), l. 19, and 'Greater Love' (p. 53), l. 6.
  25 flound'ring: Cp. letter of 16 January 1917 quoted above: 'I was
      mercifully helped to do my duty and crawl, wade, climb, and flounder
      over No Man's Land to visit my other post' (CL, 427–8).
  28 one: Cp. letter quoted above: 'I nearly broke down and let myself drown
      in the water that was now slowly rising over my knees' (CL, 427).

CP&F, 371

SMILE, SMILE, SMILE

Head to limp head, the sunk-eyed wounded scanned
Yesterday's *Mail*; the casualties (typed small)
And (large) Vast Booty from our Latest Haul.
Also, they read of Cheap Homes, not yet planned,
5   'For', said the paper, 'when this war is done
The men's first instincts will be making homes.
Meanwhile their foremost need is aerodromes,
It being certain war has but begun.
Peace would do wrong to our undying dead, –
10 The sons we offered might regret they died
If we got nothing lasting in their stead.
We must be solidly indemnified.
Though all be worthy Victory which all bought,
We rulers sitting in this ancient spot
15 Would wrong our very selves if we forgot
The greatest glory will be theirs who fought,
Who kept this nation in integrity.'
Nation? – The half-limbed readers did not chafe
But smiled at one another curiously
20 Like secret men who know their secret safe.
(This is the thing they know and never speak,
That England one by one had fled to France,
Not many elsewhere now, save under France.)
Pictures of these broad smiles appear each week,
25 And people in whose voice real feeling rings
Say: How they smile! They're happy now, poor things.

Written in France in mid- to late September 1918 (WO, 273–4). On 22
September, WO wrote to SS: 'Did you see what the Minister of Labour said in
the *Mail* the other day? "The first instincts of the men after the cessation of
hostilities will be to return home." And again – "All classes acknowledge their
indebtedness to the soldiers & sailors . . ."

   'About the same day, Clemenceau is reported by *The Times* as saying: "All are
worthy . . . yet we should be untrue to ourselves if we forgot that the greatest
glory will be to the splendid poilus, who, etc."

   'I began a Postscript to these Confessions, but hope you will already have
lashed yourself, (lashed yourself!) into something . . .' (CL, 578) *The Times* of 19
September 1918 had reported the French premier as saying: 'All are worthy of
victory, because they will know how to honour it. Yet, however, in the ancient

spot where sit the fathers of the Republic we should be untrue to ourselves if we forgot that the greatest glory will be to those splendid *poilus* [French slang for 'common soldiers'] who will see confirmed by history the titles of nobility which they themselves have earned. At the present moment they ask for nothing more than to be allowed to complete the great work which will assure them of immortality. What do they want and what do you? To keep on fighting victoriously until the moment when the enemy will understand there is no possible negotiation between crime and right.'

TITLE   Taken from one of the most popular British songs on the Western Front, which begins:
   What's the use of worrying?
      It never was worth while,
   So, pack up your troubles in your old kit-bag
      And smile, smile, smile.

CP&F, 374

SPRING OFFENSIVE

Halted against the shade of a last hill
They fed, and eased of pack-loads, were at ease;
And leaning on the nearest chest or knees
Carelessly slept.
                    But many there stood still
5   To face the stark blank sky beyond the ridge,
Knowing their feet had come to the end of the world.
Marvelling they stood, and watched the long grass swirled
By the May breeze, murmurous with wasp and midge;
And though the summer oozed into their veins
10   Like an injected drug for their bodies' pains,
Sharp on their souls hung the imminent ridge of grass,
Fearfully flashed the sky's mysterious glass.

Hour after hour they ponder the warm field
And the far valley behind, where buttercups
15   Had blessed with gold their slow boots coming up;
When even the little brambles would not yield
But clutched and clung to them like sorrowing arms.
They breathe like trees unstirred.

Till like a cold gust thrills the little word
20   At which each body and its soul begird
And tighten them for battle. No alarms
Of bugles, no high flags, no clamorous haste, –
Only a lift and flare of eyes that faced
The sun, like a friend with whom their love is done.
25   O larger shone that smile against the sun, –
Mightier than his whose bounty these have spurned.

So, soon they topped the hill, and raced together
Over an open stretch of herb and heather
Exposed. And instantly the whole sky burned
30   With fury against them; earth set sudden cups
In thousands for their blood; and the green slope
Chasmed and deepened sheer to infinite space.

Of them who running on that last high place

Breasted the surf of bullets, or went up
35 On the hot blast and fury of hell's upsurge,
Or plunged and fell away past this world's verge,
Some say God caught them even before they fell.

But what say such as from existence' brink
Ventured but drave too swift to sink,
40 The few who rushed in the body to enter hell,
And there out-fiending all its fiends and flames
With superhuman inhumanities,
Long-famous glories, immemorial shames –
And crawling slowly back, have by degrees
45 Regained cool peaceful air in wonder –
Why speak not they of comrades that went under?

Begun probably at Scarborough in July 1918, this poem was revised in France in
mid- to late September (WO, 274–6). A fair copy of ll. 1–17 was sent with WO's
letter of 22 September 1918 to SS. An accompanying note asked: 'Is this worth
going on with? I don't want to write anything to which a soldier would say No
Compris!' (CU) There is no evidence that SS replied. The poem draws on WO's
experience of the Allies' 'spring offensive' in April 1917 (WO, 178–82), and its
MSS show that it was never finally revised.

  2–3 Previous editors read: 'They fed, and lying easy, were at ease / And,
        finding comfortable chests and knees,'

   11 ridge: Previous editors read 'line'.

  14–15 buttercups: Previous editors read 'the buttercup'. WO had coined the
          image of l. 15 in 1907, returning through the fields to Shrewsbury after
          Evensong in Uffington Church. HO remembered: 'Wilfred gently
          pressed my arm for silence – hesitated a moment and then called quietly
          back, "Harold's boots are blessed with gold"' (JFO, 1. 176). The image
          subsequently appeared in 'A Palinode' (JS, 54), ll. 17–20:
              But if the sovereign sun I might behold
              With condescension coming down benign,
              And blessing all the field and air with gold,
              Then the contentment of the world was mine.
          Cp. also Keats, 'To Autumn', ll. 2–4:
              Close bosom-friend of the maturing sun;
              Conspiring with him how to load and bless
              With fruit the vines that round the thatch-eaves run . . .

   16 When: Previous editors read 'Where'.

   17 arms: Previous editors read 'hands'.

18 The MS reads: '~~All they strange day~~ they breathe like trees unstirred', and one must suppose that WO intended to find alternatives for the cancelled words.

23–5 Cp. WO to CO, 14 May 1917: 'And his face shone with the brightness of the sun' (CL, 459).

29–31 Cp. Henri Barbusse, *Under Fire* (1917), 244: 'Abruptly, across all the width of the opposite slope, lurid flames burst forth that strike the air with terrible detonations. In line from left to right fires emerge from the sky and explosions from the ground.'

30 DH notes 'The word *cups* suggests not only shell-holes but also *buttercup[s]* (l. 14) and chalices, cups which are used in the Mass to contain the wine which is both a blessing (cf. *blessed with gold*) and sacrificial blood. Having refused the offered blessing of communion with the natural order, the men have become victims sacrificed to an outraged Nature.' (DH, 135) Dr Ellen Sarot has detected an echo of Genesis 4: 10–11: 'The voice of thy brother's blood crieth unto me from the ground. And now art thou cursed from the earth, which hath opened her mouth to receive thy brother's blood from thy hand . . .'

33 last high place: 'another reference to sacrifice – hilltop sacrificial altars were known in ancient times as "high places"' (DH, 135).

34 Previous editors read: 'Leapt to swift unseen bullets, or went up'. EB misread 'surf' as 'swift'. Of the variant, and mainly cancelled, forms of this line (see transcript on CP&F, 378), I prefer one first proposed by Welland.

CP&F, 376

THE FRAGMENTS

[AN IMPERIAL ELEGY]

1   Not one corner of a foreign field
But a span as wide as Europe;
An appearance of a titan's grave,
And the length thereof a thousand miles,
It crossed all Europe like a mystic road,
Or as the Spirits' Pathway lieth on the night.
And I heard a voice crying
2   This is the Path of Glory.

Written sometime between September 1915 and the early summer of 1916. The fragment 'Purgatorial Passions' (CP&F, 455), which is on identical paper, carries a marginal note, 'How to Instruct in Aiming and Firing', the title of a military manual, which suggests that this fragment was written during one of the musketry courses WO took in 1916. On 1 August 1914 he had told SO: 'I made the mistake the other day, of striking the opening bars of *Marche Funèbre*, since when [Nénette Léger] pesters me daily for more' (CL, 272). EB, 122; CDL.

1   Cp. Rupert Brooke, 'The Soldier', l. 2: 'there's some corner of a foreign field'. WO owned a copy of Brooke's *1914 & Other Poems* (13th imp., 1916).

2   Cp. Gray, 'Elegy Written in a Country Churchyard', l. 36: 'The paths of glory lead but to the grave.'

[I KNOW THE MUSIC]

1 All sounds have been as music to my listening:
2   Pacific lamentations of slow bells,
    The crunch of boots on blue snow rosy-glistening,
      Shuffle of autumn leaves; and all farewells:

3 Bugles that sadden all the evening air,
     And country bells clamouring their last appeals
    Before [the] music of the evening prayer;
4   Bridges, sonorous under carriage wheels.

    Gurgle of sluicing surge through hollow rocks,
     The gluttonous lapping of the waves on weeds,
    Whisper of grass; the myriad-tinkling flocks,
     The warbling drawl of flutes and shepherds' reeds.

    The orchestral noises of October nights
     Blowing [   ] symphonetic storms
    Of startled clarions [   ]
     Drums, rumbling and rolling thunderous and [ ].

    Thrilling of throstles in the keen blue dawn,
5   Bees fumbling and fuming over sainfoin-fields.

Written at Craiglockhart in late August or early September 1917, this fragmentary poem would seem to owe its catalogue structure to Rupert Brooke, 'The Great Lover' (quoted in WO to SO, 18 March 1917 [CL, 443]), and may have been abandoned after WO had drawn on its diction for 'Anthem for Doomed Youth' (p. 12). EB, CDL, DH.

1 Cp. SS, 'Alone', ll. 1–2: 'I've listened: and all the sounds I heard / Were music.'

2 Cp. 'A Palinode' (JS, 54), l. 45: 'Pacific lamentations of a bell', and Flaubert, *Madame Bovary*, part II, chap. VI: 'et la cloche, sonnant toujours, continuait dans les airs sa lamentation pacifique'.

3 Cp. 'Anthem for Doomed Youth', l.8: 'And bugles calling for them from sad shires'.

4 Cp. 'A Palinode', l. 44: 'Bridges, sonorous under rapid wheels'.

5 sainfoin: a herb grown for fodder.

CP&F, 485–6

BUT I WAS LOOKING AT THE PERMANENT STARS

1   Bugles sang, saddening the evening air,
     And bugles answered, sorrowful to hear.

     Voices of boys were by the river-side.
     Sleep mothered them; and left the twilight sad.
     The shadow of the morrow weighed on men.

     Voices of old despondency resigned,
     Bowed by the shadow of the morrow, slept.

     [   ] dying tone
     Of receding voices that will not return.
     The wailing of the high far-travelling shells
     And the deep cursing of the provoking [   ].

2   The monstrous anger of our taciturn guns.
     The majesty of the insults of their mouths.

Written at Craiglockhart in late August 1917 shortly before WO read the
anonymous Prefatory Note to *Poems of Today: an Anthology* (1916), that triggered
'Anthem for Doomed Youth' (p. 12), for which poem these fragments may
almost be considered preliminary drafts. EB (entitled 'Voices'), CDL, DH (both
entitled 'Bugles Sang').
   1   Cp. the fragment, 'I know the music' (p. 84): Bugles that sadden all the
       evening air'; also 'Anthem for Doomed Youth', l. 8: 'And bugles calling
       for them from sad shires'.
   2   Cp. 'Anthem for Doomed Youth', l. 2: '– Only the monstrous anger of
       the guns'.

CP&F, 487–8

BEAUTY

The beautiful, the fair, the elegant,
1   Is that which pleases us, says Kant,
Without a thought of interest or advantage.

I used to watch men when they spoke of beauty
And measure their enthusiasm. One
An old man, seeing a [   ] setting sun,
Praised it [   ] a certain sense of duty
To the calm evening and his time of life.
I know another man that never says a Beauty
But of a horse; [   ]

Men seldom speak of beauty, beauty as such,
Not even lovers think about it much.
Women of course consider it for hours
In mirrors; [   ]

A shrapnel ball –
Just where the wet skin glistened when he swam –
Like a full-opened sea-anemone.
2   We both said 'What a beauty! What a beauty, lad!'
I knew that in that flower he saw a hope
Of living on, and seeing again the roses of his home.
Beauty is that which pleases and delights,
Not bringing personal advantage – Kant.
But later on I heard
A canker worked into that crimson flower
And that he sank with it
And laid it with the anemones off Dover.

Written at Craiglockhart, probably in September 1917. WO may have been
remembering an event described in his letter of 6 [?8] April 1917 to SO:
'Another night I was putting out an Advanced Post when we were seen or
heard and greeted with Shrapnel. The man crouching shoulder to shoulder to
me gets a beautiful round hole deep in his biceps.' (CL, 450) EB (Notes, 129),
CDL.

1   Cp. Immanuel Kant, *The Critique of Judgement* (trans. James Creed
    Meredith, Oxford, 1928), l. 1. i, 'Analytic of the Beautiful', First
    Moment, 5:

A vague pearl, a wan pearl
You showed me once; I peered through far-gone winters
Until my mind was fog-bound in that gem.

Blue diamonds, cold diamonds
You shook before me, so that out of them
Glittered and glowed vast diamond dawns of spring.

Tiger-eyed rubies, wrathful rubies
You rolled. I watched their hot hearts fling
Flames from each glaring summer of my life.

Quiet amber, mellow amber
You lifted; and behold the whole air rife
With evening, and the auburn autumn cloud.

But pale skin, your pearl skin
Show this to me, and I shall have surprise
Of every snow-lit dawn before it break.

But clear eyes, your fresh eyes
Open; that I may laugh, and lightly take
All air of early April in one hour.

But brown curls, O shadow me with curls,
Full of September mist, half-gleam, half-glower,
And I shall roam warm nights in lands far south.

'The *agreeable* is what GRATIFIES a man; the *beautiful* what simply PLEASES
him; the *good* what is ESTEEMED (approved), i.e. that on which he sets an
objective worth . . . Of all these three kinds of delight, that of taste in the
beautiful may be said to be the one and only disinterested and *free*
delight;
for, with it, no interest, whether of sense or reason, extorts approval.'

2   The wound is said to be a beauty because it is seen to be a 'blighty', a
soldiers' slang term for one serious enough for the sufferer to be sent
back to 'Blighty' (England).

Then in an instant from your mouth
Give me the fury of noondays and the sum
Of the fulness of summers yet to come.

Drafted, probably in mid-November 1917, when WO was staying at the
Regent Palace Hotel (CL, 506–7). He may have abandoned this poem after
drawing on its diction for the more successful one beginning 'I saw his round
mouth's crimson deepen as it fell' (p. 17).

　　CDL prints the first three stanzas only.

　1　Graham Holliday detects an echo of Keats, 'Had I a man's fair form',
　　　l. 14: 'I'll gather some spells, and incantation.'

CP&F, 494–6

[CRAMPED IN THAT FUNNELLED HOLE]

1   Cramped in that funnelled hole, they watched the dawn
    Open a jagged rim around; a yawn
    Of death's jaws, which had all but swallowed them
2   Stuck in the bottom of his throat of phlegm.

3   They were in one of many mouths of Hell
    Not seen of seers in visions, only felt
    As teeth of traps; when bones and the dead are smelt
    Under the mud where long ago they fell
    Mixed with the sour sharp odour of the shell.

Written at Scarborough, probably on 4 December 1917. The previous day WO had written to SO: 'I'm going to get up at dawn tomorrow to do a dawn piece which I've had in mind since those dismal hours at York, 3 to 7 a.m.! All dressed up, and nowhere to go.' (CL, 513) (See DH, 'The Date of Wilfred Owen's "Exposure"', N&Q, n.s., xxiii, no. 7 [July 1976], 305–8, for a discussion of the linked roots of that poem and this.) 'Cramped in that funnelled hole' was prompted by WO's reading of Tennyson (WO, 248 and 321) and Barbusse (CL, 520). Like such other of WO's visions of the descent into Hell as 'Deep under turfy grass and heavy clay (JS, 39), 'Uriconium' (p. 3), and 'The Show' (p. 42), the hole or tunnel is described in physical terms. EB, CDL, DH.

1 Cp. 'Mental Cases' (p. 56), l. 22: 'Dawn breaks open like a wound that bleeds afresh.'

2 Cp. Henri Barbusse, *Under Fire* (1917), 126: 'The soldier held his peace. In the distance he saw the night as *they* would pass it – cramped up, trembling with vigilance in the deep darkness, at the bottom of the listening-hole whose ragged jaws showed in black outline all around whenever a gun hurled its dawn into the sky.'

3 Cp. Tennyson, 'The Charge of the Light Brigade', ll. 24–6: 'Into the jaws of Death, / Into the mouth of Hell / Rode the six hundred.'

CP&F, 511–13

THE WRESTLERS

So neck to neck and obstinate knee to knee
Wrestled those two; and peerless Heracles
Could not prevail nor catch at any vantage;
But those huge hands which small had strangled snakes
Let slip the writhing of Antaeas' wrists;
Those clubs of hands that wrenched the necks of bulls
Now fumbled round the slim Antaeas' limbs
Baffled. Then anger swelled in Heracles,
And terribly he grappled broader arms,
And yet more firmly fixed his grasping feet,
And up his back the muscles bulged and shone
Like climbing banks and domes of towering cloud.
Many who watched that wrestling say he laughed, –
1 But not so loud as on Eurystheus of old,
But that his pantings, seldom loosed, long pent,
Were like the sighs of lions at their meat.
Men say their fettered fury tightened hour by hour,
Until the veins rose tubrous on their brows
And froth flew thickly-shivered from both beards.
As pythons shudder, bridling-in their spite,
So trembled that Antaeas with held strength,
While Heracles, – the thews and cordage of his thighs
Straitened and strained beyond the utmost stretch
From quivering heel to haunch like sweating hawsers –
But only staggered backward. Then his throat
Growled, like a great beast when his meat is touched,
As if he smelt some guile behind Antaeas,
And knew the buttressed bulking of his shoulders
Bore not the mass to move it one thumb's length.
But what it was so helped the man none guessed,
2 Save Hylas, whom the fawns had once made wise
How earth herself empowered him by her touch,
Gave him the grip and stringency of winter,
3 And all the ardour of the invincible spring;
How all the blood of June glutted his heart;
And the wild glow of huge autumnal storms
Stirred on his face, and flickered from his eyes;
How, too, Poseidon blessed him fatherly

[90]

With wafts of vigour from the keen sea waves,
And with the subtle coil of currents –
Strange underflows, that maddened Heracles.
And towards the night they sundered, neither thrown.
Whereat came Hylas running to his friend
With fans, and sponges in a laving-bowl,
And brimmed his lord the beakerful he loved,
Which Heracles took roughly, even from him.
Then spake that other from the place he stood:
'O Heracles, I know thy fights and labours,
What man thou wert, and what thou art become,
The lord of strength, queller of perilous monsters,
Hero of heroes, worthy immortal worship,
But me thou canst not quell. For I, I come
Of Earth, and to my father Poseidon,
Whose strength ye know, and whose displeasure ye know.
Therefore be wise, and try me not again,
But say thou findst me peer, and more than peer.'
But Heracles, of utter weariness,
Was loath to answer, either yea or nay.
And a cruel murmur rankled through the crowd.
Now he whose knees propped up the head of him,
Over his lord's ear swiftly whispered thus:
'If thou could'st lift the man in air – enough.
His feet suck secret virtue of the earth.
Lift him, and buckle him to thy breast, and win.'
Up sprang the son of Perseus deeply laughing
And ere the crimson of his last long clutch
Had faded from that insolent's throat, again
4   They closed. Then he, the Argonaut,
Remembering how he tore the oaks in Argos,
Bound both his arms about the other's loins
And with a sudden tugging, easily
Rooted him up; and crushed his inmost bones.
Forth to the town he strode, and through the streets,
Bearing the body light as leopard-skins,
And glorious ran the shouting as he strode –
Some say his footfalls made an earthquake there
So that he dropped Antaeas: some say not:
But that he cast him down by Gea's altar

And Gea sent that earthquake for her son,
To rouse him out of death. And lo! he röse,
Alive, and came to Heracles
Who feasted with the people and their King.
And fain would all make place for him
But he would not consent. And Heracles,
Knowing the hate of Hylas for his deeds,
Feasted and slept; and so forgot the man,
And early on the morrow passed with Hylas
Down to the Argo, for the wind was fair.

Drafted at Craiglockhart in July 1917, in response to a suggestion by Dr
Arthur John Brock, one of the three medical officers at the hospital (WO,
196–7). Under the pseudonym 'Arcturus', he wrote an article for *The Hydra*
(January 1918), entitled 'Antaeus, or Back to the Land', which ended:
'Antaeus was a young Libyan giant, whose parents were Gaia and Poseidon,
Earth and Sea. In a wrestling combat he could not be overthrown as long as
his feet were on his Mother Earth. When he was raised off the earth his
strength rapidly failed, only to be renewed again at the first contact with the
soil. Finally, Hercules, seeing this, lifted him bodily up in the air, and holding
him there, crushed him to death in his arms.
    'Now surely every officer who comes to Craiglockhart recognises that, in a
way, he is himself Antaeus who has been taken from his Mother Earth and
well-nigh crushed to death by the war giant or military machine . . . Antaeus
typifies the occupation cure at Craiglockhart. His story is the justification of
our activities.'
    On [?14] July 1917, WO wrote to SO: 'On the Hercules-Antaeus Subject –
there are only 3 or 4 lines in the Dictionaries. So I shall just do a Sonnet' (CL,
476). On the 17th, he incorporated 14 lines from the poem in another letter
to SO, adding: 'About 50 lines are now done' (CL, 477). Some days later, he
wrote to ELG: 'last week I wrote (to order) a strong bit of Blank: on <u>Antaeus</u>
<u>v. Heracles</u>. These are the best lines, methinks: (N.B. Antaeus deriving
strength from his Mother Earth nearly licked old Herk.)
    . . . How Earth herself empowered him with her touch,
    Gave him the grip and stringency of winter,
    And all the ardour of th' invincible Spring;
    How all the blood of June glutted his heart.
    And all the glow of huge autumnal storms
    Stirred on his face, and flickered from his eyes.' (CL, 478)

Brock's article on Antaeus in *The Hydra* is followed by the editorial
announcement that 'our late Editor, Mr Owen, has reduced the Antaeus saga
to blank verse. This poem we hope to print in our next number.' On 20
December 1917, WO had written to SO of a visit to Edinburgh: 'I saw Dr.
Brock, whose first word was "Antaeas!" which they want immediately for the

next Mag! Shall have to spin it off again while up here' (CL, 517–18). WO's latest revisions date from this time. No copy of the February 1918 issue of *The Hydra* has come to light, but there is no evidence that the poem was ever finished and it seems unlikely to have been published in part during WO's lifetime. (See DH, 'A Sociological Cure for Shellshock: Dr Brock and Wilfred Owen', *Sociological Review*, xxv, no. 2 [May 1977], 377–86, for a perceptive discussion of Brock's influence on WO in general, and on this poem in particular.) CDL, DH (both print only the 14 lines incorporated in WO's letter of 17 July 1917).

1   Seeking purification for killing his wife and children, Herakles (or Hercules) spent 12 years at the court of King Eurystheus of Tiryns, during which time he performed 12 arduous labours.

2   Hylas, a beautiful youth, was a favourite companion of Herakles. WO wrote 'fawns', almost certainly a misspelling of 'fauns'.

3   Cp. 'Exposure' (p. 71), l. 33: 'For God's invincible spring our love is made afraid'.

4   Herakles was an Argonaut, one of the band of heroes that sailed with Jason in the *Argo* in search of the Golden Fleece.

CP&F, 520–5

WILD WITH ALL REGRETS
(To S.S.)

My arms have mutinied against me, – brutes!
My fingers fidget like ten idle brats,
My back's been stiff for hours, damned hours.
Death never gives his squad a Stand-at-ease.
I can't read. There: it's no use. Take your book.
A short life and a merry one, my buck!
We said we'd hate to grow dead-old. But now,
Not to live old seems awful: not to renew
My boyhood with my boys, and teach 'em hitting,
Shooting and hunting, – and all the arts of hurting!
– Well, that's what I learnt. That, and making money.
3 Your fifty years in store seem none too many,
But I've five minutes. God! For just two years
To help myself to this good air of yours!
One Spring! Is one too hard to spare? Too long?
Spring air would find its own way to my lung,
And grow me legs as quick as lilac-shoots.

*   *   *

Yes, there's the orderly. He'll change the sheets
When I'm lugged out. Oh, couldn't I do that?
Here in this coffin of a bed, I've thought
I'd like to kneel and sweep his floors for ever, –
And ask no nights off when the bustle's over,
For I'd enjoy the dirt. Who's prejudiced
Against a grimed hand when his own's quite dust, –
Less live than specks that in the sun-shafts turn?
Dear dust – in rooms, on roads, on faces' tan!
4 I'd love to be a sweep's boy, black as Town;
Yes, or a muck-man. Must I be his load?
A flea would do. If one chap wasn't bloody,
Or went stone-cold, I'd find another body.

*   *   *

Which I shan't manage now. Unless it's yours.
I shall stay in you, friend, for some few hours.
You'll feel my heavy spirit chill your chest,
And climb your throat, on sobs, until it's chased
On sighs, and wiped from off your lips by wind.
I think on your rich breathing, brother, I'll be weaned
To do without what blood remained me from my wound.

Written at Scarborough on 5 December 1917, this poem was expanded into
'A Terre', p. 65. SS, EB, CDL.

1   Cp. Tennyson, 'Tears, idle tears, I know not what they mean', ll. 19–20:
    'Deep as first love, and wild with all regret; / O Death in Life, the days
    that are no more.'

2   On the MS, the dedication to Siegfried Sassoon is followed by an
    asterisk. A matching asterisk at the foot of the page is followed by the
    question: 'May I?'

3   Cp. A. E. Housman, 'Loveliest of trees, the cherry now', ll. 9–12:
        And since to look at things in bloom
        Fifty springs are little room,
        About the woodland I will go
        To see the cherry hung with snow.

4   sweep: chimney-sweep.

CP&F, 355–6

[AS BRONZE MAY BE MUCH BEAUTIFIED]

As bronze may be much beautified
By lying in the dark damp soil,
So men who fade in dust of warfare fade
Fairer, and sorrow blooms their soul.

Like pearls which noble women wear
And, tarnishing, awhile confide
Unto the old salt sea to feed,
Many return more lustrous than they were.

But what of them buried profound,
Buried where we can no more find,
Who [   ]
1 Lie dark for ever under abysmal war?

Written at Scarborough in July 1918, this fragment is a development of another.
EB, CDL, DH.

1 Cp. WO to SS, 1 September 1918: 'Serenity Shelley never dreamed of
crowns me. Will it last when I shall have gone into Caverns & Abysmals
such as he never reserved for his worst daemons?' (CL, 571)

CP&F, 529–30

[THE ROADS ALSO]

The roads also have their wistful rest,
When the weather-cocks perch still and roost
And the looks of men turn kind to clocks
1 And the trams go empty to their drome.
　　　The streets also dream their dreams.

The old houses muse of the old days
And their fond trees lean on them and doze.
On their steps chatter and clatter stops
For the cries of other times hold men
　　　And they hear the unknown moan.

They remember alien ardours and far futures
And the smiles not seen in happy features.
Their begetters call them from the gutters;
In the gardens unborn child-souls wail,
2 　　　And the dead scribble on walls.

Though their own child cry for them in tears,
Women weep but hear no sound upstairs.
The[y] believe in love they ha[ve] not lived
And passion past the reach of stairs
　　　To the world's towers or stars.

Written at Scarborough in July–August 1918, this fragment probably owes
something to an experience described in a letter to SO of 18 February 1918:
'Last night I took an artist johnny – called [Emile] Claus ... to the
Scarborough, where there's not a house built since 1780, not a street much
wider than Claus, and miles of it, mind you, miles of glorious eighteenth
century. It was twilight and the Sunday evening bell.
　'Not a soul in the alleys.
　'Not a lamp lit. A dim moon – and the Past.
　'And we got excited. What excited us, who shall say? We jumped about, we
bumped about, we sang praises, we cursed Manchester; we looked in at half
open doors and blessed the people inside. We saw Shakespeare in a lantern,
and the whole of Italy in a Balcony. A tall chimney became a Greek Column;
and in the inscriptions on the walls we read romances and philosophies.' (CL,
533). EB and CDL print as a poem rather than a fragment. There is an earlier
draft of stanzas 1–3, which those editors conflate with the later.

PREFACE

This book is not about heroes. English poetry is not yet fit to speak of them.

1   Nor is it about deeds, or lands, nor anything about glory, honour, might, majesty, dominion, or power, except War.

Above all I am not concerned with Poetry.

My subject is War, and the pity of War.

The Poetry is in the pity.

2   Yet these elegies are to this generation in no sense consolatory. They may be to the next. All a poet can do today is warn. That is why the true Poets must be truthful.

(If I thought the letter of this book would last, I might have used proper names; but if the spirit of it survives – survives Prussia – my ambition and those names will have achieved fresher fields than Flanders . . . .)

At Ripon, probably in May 1918, WO began this draft Preface for a collection of war poems that he hoped to publish in 1919 (WO, 265–6).

1   Cp. the General Epistle of Jude 25. 'To the only wise God our Saviour, be glory and majesty, dominion and power, both now and ever.'

2   WO had considered – and decided against – calling his book *English Elegies*.

CP&F, 535

---

1   drome: garage.

2   Cp. Blake, 'London', ll. 11–16:
    And the hapless Soldier's sigh
    Runs in blood down Palace walls.

    But most thro' midnight streets I hear
    How the youthful Harlot's curse
    Blasts the new born Infant's tear,
    And blights with plagues the Marriage hearse.

CP&F. 531–2

INDEX OF TITLES AND FIRST LINES